FACING THE FIRE

As children, most of us learn that if someone gets angry, someone also gets hurt. It is an equation that quickly teaches us to run away from anger. But John Lee provides a new equation: *Anger, when felt and expressed appropriately, equals energy, intimacy, and serenity.* Here, in *Facing the Fire*, John Lee shows you how to face your anger . . . to examine what you're feeling, to figure out what type of anger has you in its grip, and to choose the best technique for expressing that anger. It is an invaluable process that can help improve your health and emotional well-being and enhance the lives of those you love.

PRAISE FOR
AT MY FATHER'S WEDDING

"[A] healing book. By telling his story honestly, John helps us all understand our own stories better. . . . This is a down-to-earth book that will benefit men and women." —Dr. Shepherd Bliss, professor of men's studies, JFK University

"I was deeply moved by *At My Father's Wedding*. John writes with honesty and compassion and insight about masculine consciousness. This book is a major contribution and a must read for both men and women." —Wayne Kritsberg, author of *The Adult Children of Alcoholics Syndrome*

Facing the Fire

Experiencing and Expressing Anger Appropriately

John Lee
with
Bill Stott

BANTAM BOOKS

NEW YORK · TORONTO · LONDON
SYDNEY · AUCKLAND

Facing the Fire
A Bantam Book / July 1993

Library of Congress Cataloging-in-Publication Data
Lee, John H., 1951–
Facing the fire : experiencing and expressing your anger
appropriately
John Lee, with Bill Stott.
p. cm.
ISBN 978-0-553-37240-3 (pbk.) :
1. Anger. 2. Behavior therapy. 3. Behavior modification.
I. Stott, William, 1940– . II. Title.
BF575.A5L44 1993
152.4'7—dc20   92-46216
                                                    CIP
Published simultaneously in the United States and Canada

Bantam Books are published by Bantam Books, a division of Bantam Doubleday Dell Publishing Group, Inc. Its trademark, con-
sisting of the words "Bantam Books" and the portrayal of a rooster,
is Registered in U.S. Patent and Trademark Office and in other
countries. Marca Registrada. Bantam Books, New York, New York.

PRINTED IN THE UNITED STATES OF AMERICA

John Lee's dedication: This book is for my
friend Dan Jones, with whom I learned much
of what's in it.

Bill Stott's dedication: This book is for the giants
of my youth—especially those who showed me
how to love life.

"Ma'am, I was full of fire. I had to carry fire insurance till I was forty."
—W. C. Fields

Contents

Introduction

We human beings naturally want love. Most of us don't actively seek out people or situations that sadden, frustrate, or anger us. But the human condition doesn't provide for only the bright emotions, love, hope, and happiness, without a serving of the dark side of the human psyche as well, pain, despair, and anger.

As children, we learned to associate anger with pain when angry people, usually angry adults, caused us to feel pain. So as adults, most of us usually do all we can to avoid or deny anger, especially the anger we feel inside us. Because we learned that anger leads to pain, we became afraid of anger. We don't want to feel any more pain, and we don't want to cause pain for others. Our fear of anger is so great that we can't believe that our own anger is okay, and we can't believe it's as natural as the other emotions we have, or that we can learn to express it in safe, healthy, and appropriate ways.

But we can—and we must. Because pent-up anger is unhealthy; it's bad for us and for the people around us. Pent-up anger keeps us from enjoying life, keeps us from being genuinely ourselves with the people we love, keeps us from having open, comfortable relationships with our friends and associates.

As this book will show you, anger can be expressed so safely and completely that it leads not to pain but to strength, to increased energy, to deeper communication with those we value, and to personal serenity.

We must stop hurting ourselves, one another, and our children with our anger and other pent-up emotions. This book tells how.

After I finished editing the final version of this book, I felt the way I expect a father feels when he sees his child dressed and ready for the first day of school: proud and a bit sad. I'd lived with this book a long time, and now it was time to send it out into the world.

I turned on the TV. TV is my last addiction. I've given up cigarettes, alcohol, drugs, red meat, fried foods, and suffering, but I can't give up the box. Oprah Winfrey was on, looking serious. Six men and women were confessing that they abused their children. They were embarrassed and ashamed, and they were pleading for someone to tell them what to do, how to stop. All the abusers had themselves been abused as children, and they wove together stories of what had happened to them as children with stories of what they were doing to their kids now. Some of the stories could have been told by my mother and father. Or me.

These parents were not intentionally bad or malicious, but they were hurting their children and they knew it. They kept talking about how ''anger'' and ''rage'' would build up in them until it couldn't be ''contained'' and suddenly ''exploded'' out. They'd scream at their children, verbally abuse them. One mother had told her daughter, ''I wish you were dead''; the mother hid her face in her hand as she admitted this. They had all hit, beaten, or whipped their children. The story that made me saddest was the one told by a mother who said she'd listened to her baby cry for several hours and, finally unable to stand it, had picked him up from the crib and shaken him into silence.

By the time *Oprah* was over, *I* was shaking. No one on the show had helped those parents. No one knew what to tell them except ''You've got to control yourself.''

But they'd tried to do that, and it hadn't worked!

I knew how to help those people. I knew that their problem wasn't "controlling" the anger: it was expressing it safely—getting it out in a way that wouldn't do any harm. Seeing that *Oprah* program made me realize how important this book is.

For more than seven years I had been lecturing and giving workshops on anger and selling tapes of these sessions. I had been around people in the recovery community and around men who were committed to learning to feel and express their emotions in ways that didn't hurt others. I had come to take for granted that people knew how to handle their anger appropriately.

But the people on *Oprah* didn't. And if their worried faces were any indication, the people in Oprah's audience didn't, either. I suddenly realized how few of us do know how to cope with our anger. I remembered how I'd gone down on my knees and thanked God when I first understood that I had the knowledge and tools for releasing my anger in a healthy way.

That's what I'm going to give you in this book: the knowledge that you can feel your anger and not be afraid of it; that you can face your anger and deal with it mentally, emotionally, and—most important—physically; *and* that you can express and release your anger, get it out of your system, in safe, nonthreatening, nonhurtful ways that will ultimately enable you to be a happier, healthier person.

So please, stick with me through this process. It's a gradual one, and I'll go with you step-by-step. I promise you that you'll be a lot more comfortable with yourself and other people when you've heard what I have to say and tried out the methods I suggest. I'm going to tell you something that may change your life. I'm going to tell you how to deal with your anger—however strong it is, even if it's rage or beyond rage—and get it out of your body in a way that won't hurt you, or your body or soul, or the body or soul of anyone you care about or of *anyone* else.

ANGER AND YOU

In this book,

- I suggest that you shouldn't be afraid of your anger or try to escape it, because you can't.

- I say that the right thing to do with your anger (and every other emotion) is to *feel* it.
- I give you safe and healthy ways to face your anger, and feel and express it both by yourself and with other people.
- I suggest that feeling and expressing your anger in safe ways will improve your physical and spiritual health and your intimacy with people you care about.

Other people have already said what I say in this book. A few people use these ideas, as I do, in individual counseling and in workshops on anger. But much of what I say goes against the commonly held ideas about anger. As I will explain, my view on how to deal with anger contradicts the recommendations of popular books like Carol Tavris's *Anger: The Misunderstood Emotion* (1982), Harriet Goldhor Lerner's *The Dance of Anger* (1985), and Gayle Rosellini and Mark Worden's *Of Course You're Angry* (1985). These books, good though they are in many ways, are wrong in arguing that anger is an emotion that we can successfully deal with by "understanding" it.

They are wrong because anger isn't an idea—it's a feeling. Like other feelings, anger doesn't happen in your head; it happens in your body. Because it is a feeling in your body, anger doesn't disappear when you have intellectually understood what causes it. Anger goes only when your body has expressed it—literally pushed it out.

What I say in this book may seem obvious once I've said it. To some readers, it will seem unsophisticated. I can only reply that anger and the other emotions are indeed obvious, unsophisticated, even primitive, and that, to be healthy, we have to deal with them as they are.

In emphasizing the importance of physically feeling your anger, I don't mean to imply that your intelligence does not have an important role to play in dealing with anger. Your intelligence is very important. Your intelligence, after all, is *conscious* of what you feel. It can articulate what is causing anger and evaluate what is and isn't reasonable behavior for an angry person, whether that person is you or someone else. Your intelligence reads this book and mediates between my words and your feelings.

But anger can be dealt with successfully only when the mind and the body, which are more interdependent than we know, are in a balanced relationship. This balanced relationship means that both assert their rightful claims: the body to feeling and expressing feeling, and the mind to interpreting and evaluating.

Having said this, I must add that some of the things I'm going to say in this book would be unhealthy for some people to hear. So I want to make sure you are ready to join me in facing the fire.

WHO THIS BOOK IS FOR

This book is for you if you're over seventeen and—like me and most people—a walking-around, basically functional neurotic.

People like us were brought up to be "good" and "nice" and "decent" and "considerate" and to hide the parts of us that are angry and sad. We contain our anger, rage, sadness, and grief nearly all the time—hold in stuff we should let go of.

This book will tell you why we need to let it go and how we can let it go safely, so that no one gets hurt.

WHO THIS BOOK IS NOT FOR

1. Psychotics

Psychotics are people who are out of touch with reality *most* of the time. We neurotics are only out of touch with reality *some* of the time, which causes many of our mistakes and follies. How much worse our problems would be if we were as out of touch as the mentally ill.

2. Batterers and Rage-oholics

The problem for us neurotics is that we contain powerful emotions that we should let go of. The problem for batterers and rage-oholics is just the opposite: They can't contain anything. Their sense of self, of boundaries, of reality (I would say) is so weak that they are compelled to impose their "order" everywhere.

Batterers and rage-oholics have to build up their ability not to release but to contain their powerful emotions. They have to learn what is theirs and what is not theirs—learn, for example, that their anger is theirs and comes from them and not from anything in the world they can fix.

Batterers and rage-oholics and people who vent their anger on other people could be misled by what I say in this book. My ideas and exercises might be harmful to them and to those around them. I ask these people to put the book down.

3. Alcoholics and Drug Addicts

I believe the principles I am putting forward in this book apply to anyone, but alcoholics and drug addicts, like batterers and rage-oholics, are likely to have trouble applying them correctly. This is because alcoholics and drug addicts are altering their minds and moods in ways that make it difficult for them to know reality and safely lose control of it.

I am tempted to say that practicing alcoholics and drug addicts have more important things to deal with than what I'm discussing here. Whether or not that's true, I *know* they cannot safely do the exercises I give here while under the influence of drink or drugs. They are not then safe people to be around.

If you are an active alcoholic or drug addict, read the book if you choose to, but get sober before you try to apply what it says.

ANGER AND ME

Let me tell you why I think what I say about anger and you is true: Let me tell you about anger and me. For the first half of my biblical seventy years, I tried to bury my tears and anger. "Men don't cry," I was told, so I didn't cry. I didn't need to be told that anger was dangerous—I had seen it for myself. I tried everything I could think of to make my own anger go away. I spent my first fourteen years praying that things would change in my family so I could keep down the grief and rage I didn't allow myself to feel. I took in gigantic quantities of sugar, pop music, mystical books, ice cream, TV—anything that would dim my feelings down. By age sixteen I was addicted to cigarettes, alcohol, and work; by age twenty-one, to marijuana, sex, and meditation. Throughout my first thirty-five years I was a compulsive nice guy who constantly said, "Yes, sir, everything is fine, just fine; what can I do for *you*?"

But the fire wasn't extinguished. It smoldered in my dreams. I could fool myself, or try to, but not my unconscious, which nightly had me whipping and being whipped, wrestling, or shooting Commies, school bullies, or my father. My body was as filled with aggressive violence as is our nation's psyche as it is displayed in our commercial TV, movies, rock music, and sports.

More than anything I wanted to feel peaceful and serene. But I wasn't. I was seething with anger, always near to explosion. My body told me this by its constant indigestion and headaches and backaches. I didn't listen to my body: I fed it Tums and aspirin. The women I dated and loved told me this, and when I didn't listen, they left, saying my anger was a wall between us that they couldn't tear down.

How did they know I was angry when I didn't know it myself and hid it and denied it? Because no matter how hard I tried, my anger kept leaking out of me, as passive aggression, verbal abuse, withholding and withdrawing.

The last woman who left me—I call her Laural in my book *The Flying Boy*—said, "If you don't get this anger out, you're going to destroy everybody who wants to love you.'' That was a pretty frightening threat. She took it for granted that my anger was going to destroy me; she was looking *beyond* me to the others it would destroy.

When Laural left, I hit bottom. At the time, I was living in Austin, Texas, and failing to write a Ph.D. dissertation. For years I had been going to psychotherapists, trying to learn why I felt depressed and empty. The counseling had helped: It had taught me that I had reasons to feel hurt and bitter. But it didn't change the way I *felt*. It didn't bring me joy or serenity, because (I now know) you can't feel *any* of the primal emotions, even the happy ones, until you feel them *all*.

Psychotherapy gave me intellectual insights, often exciting ones, but I'd usually forget them the same day I got them. The last psychiatrist I saw, a woman, did encourage me to cry whenever I felt like it, and I cried in her presence. She supported my grieving because she had suffered a lot and knew how important it is for people to embrace their sadness. She didn't encourage me to release my anger, though. Her family had had too much rage in it for her to believe that anger can be a safe emotion. I knew something was missing.

Then one day in *New Texas,* a personal growth Austin newspaper, I saw an ad for Dan Jones, a counselor I'd heard good things about. In the ad, Dan said something like, ''If you're having trouble getting over a relationship and are tired of hurting, maybe I can help.''

Dan and I talked for several sessions about Laural's having left and my dysfunctional childhood. I was happy to talk about things as long as I didn't have to *feel* them.

Then, out of the blue, referring to something I'd just said, Dan said, ''That must make you feel sad.''

''Yeah, it does,'' I said.

''You don't look sad,'' he said. ''You've got a nice tight smile on your face. It says, 'Hey! I'm okay. This is nothing.' ''

''What do you expect me to do—start bawling?'' I said.

''If that's what you want to do,'' Dan said.

It was hard to show my emotions to a man. But the next session, I accepted his invitation: I cried a little as I talked about what hurt me. When I saw I could cry and not be shamed for it, I cried at every session.

Then, also out of the blue, Dan said something terrifying. I'll never forget it. He said, "It sounds to me like you're angry at your father for beating you and never being there for you emotionally."

"I am," I whispered, as though my father, who was a thousand miles away, might hear.

"Or—wait! No, I'm not," I said in a stronger voice. "I work hard to not be angry. I meditate to avoid it."

Dan nodded. He has this funny way of nodding, as if he totally believes what you say. "I'm probably wrong," he said. "I'd like for you to take this pillow and punch your fist into it as hard as you can and say, 'I'm angry, Dad!' "

I looked at Dan, feeling as if he had asked me to climb Mount Everest naked in an hour or less.

He dropped a thick pillow in my lap.

I was numb. I didn't know what would happen if I started punching the pillow. Would I go off the deep end? Would I follow Charlie Whitman up the University of Texas tower and start shooting? Could pounding a pillow possibly make me feel better?

Dan had told me it would. He said that what he recommended for people who couldn't access their feelings was "emotional-release work." I remembered that Laural would feel better when she got her anger out by slamming a tennis racket on the bed. I used to make fun of her and shame her as my parents had shamed me when I'd tried to express "negative" emotions like anger or grief.

I looked at the pillow for maybe a minute. I put my hands on both edges of it. Then I gave it back to Dan and said, "I can't do it. This is silly. I'm not paying good money to have you make a fool of me. What my father did was *then*. This is now. I don't see how what he did has anything to do with anything. Can't we just talk some more?"

"Sure," Dan said.

"Thanks," I said. And I started crying again.

I left Dan's office that day thinking I'd never go back. I had read about primal scream therapy, and I'd heard of therapists who had people beating pillows and yelling and kicking and crying. I didn't want to do work like that. Those ugly emotions disgusted me; to give in to them seemed uncivilized and *dumb*. Like most people, I thought that feeling those emotions wasn't necessary because if a therapist was really good, he or she could give you the insights you needed to be able to handle your life *intellectually*.

Also, I was scared. I knew at some level that I was running from my anger and was out of touch with my body. What would happen when I got in touch? I wouldn't start shooting people from the tower, I knew. But what *would* I do?

My biggest fear—and I've seen this with hundreds of people— was that I'd hurt myself. Maybe have a heart attack. I got hurt plenty as a kid. I didn't want to be hurt as an adult. That's what I liked about psychotherapy: You couldn't get hurt while sitting on a couch and talking.

I was most scared, I think, of getting out of control—you know, from pounding and shouting and hitting and kicking. All survivors of dysfunctional childhoods have a tremendous fear of losing control, partly because when we were kids and got out of control, we were punished so hard, and partly because we've seen the damage our parents did when they got out of control.

It took me two weeks to call Dan and make another appointment. I spent that time worrying. The thing that finally made me call was that I remembered that when I'd told Dan I didn't want to hit the pillow and he said I didn't have to, I'd cried. I knew there was part of me that was sad that I hadn't tried to get to my anger.

Dan began the next session by repeating that I was going to proceed at my own pace. "Whatever feels right to you is what we'll do," he said.

"I want to punch the pillow," I said.

"Hmm!" he said. "Good." And he handed the pillow to me.

I sat with it for a moment, then began jabbing my fist into it. "I'm angry, Dad," I said three or four times.

"That doesn't sound too angry," Dan said. "More like annoyance."

"I'm angry, Dad!" I said louder.

"Good—let's hear it, and see you beat the pillow."

I kept repeating that I was angry and beating the pillow and getting more and more caught up in my emotion until I was screaming and sobbing with rage and burying my fists in the pillow as hard as I could. Maybe for the first time since I was a boy, I got out of my head and into my full-bodied feeling. I broke through half a lifetime of parental teaching, social conditioning, and fear. The anger in me rose to feed my expression of it like fire leaping into a tree.

I shrieked and cried and cursed and hollered and threw my whole force into my punches. I put out enough energy to light a house, but I didn't hurt myself or Dan or anyone.

While expressing my emotion, I discovered more of what was causing it. I saw what I had been hiding from and the incidents in the past when I'd suffered my father's cruelty, my mother's helplessness. Whereas previously I'd gone home from my psychiatrist and not been able to recall what I had learned, after each session with Dan I knew: I saw that I had been abused *then,* and *then,* and *then.*

My body helped me remember. Pounding a pillow on and off for thirty minutes made my arm sore for days after; the shouting left me hoarse. Afterward, I'd realize, "My arm hurts and I can't talk too well because I'm really angry at my father. My mother, too. I'm beating them out of my system. That's what I'm doing in my work with Dan."

I left that first emotional-release session, as I was to leave all the later ones, tired but relieved. After some of the sessions I'd feel good right away. But more often, the feeling of new hope and energy came two or three hours later.

After several months I could finally believe what Dan had told me: The fire of anger is as much a God-given energy and emotion as joy, love, or sadness. I lost my fear of anger and began seeing a new and freer me emerge from my tense, dark, fearful body. My back and shoulders loosened; my chest opened up; I stood straighter but without rigidity; I walked more easily and with longer strides. I stopped having headaches and taking Tums.

Over time I came to lose my fear of my own anger and, to a healthy extent, of other people's anger. Now that I had learned what clean, appropriately expressed anger was like, I found it easy to be around. People who expressed their anger openly and correctly, I felt closer to. In a strange way their fire warmed me, as mine did them when I shared my feelings with them in a healthy way.

These days, if people are angry with me and *don't* express it, I get scared because I know that buried anger, which can turn to rage, is the most destructive emotion. Of course, if people express their anger unsafely, in a way that means to hurt me, I know to stop them or, if I can't, to get away from them and avoid them thereafter.

At bottom, what I learned from Dan is that I have the fire of anger in me and that it's a good thing.

You, reader, have the fire of anger in you. It can energize your life and bring you closer to the people you care about, as my anger has done for me. If you learn to face and feel your fire and release it properly, a new life will rise up in you like a phoenix from the ashes.

AND NOW...?

We are ready to begin.
Let us walk into the fire.

I
Your Anger and Where It Comes From

What is anger? A feeling, nothing more. A feeling like rapture or pain, boredom or peacefulness.

There is nothing wrong with anger.

This is the most difficult thing to realize about anger: There is nothing wrong with it. It's just an emotion. It is not a "negative" emotion. There are no negative emotions, though some emotions can drive us to do negative—cruel, stupid, inappropriate—things.

Christians are wrong to see anger as being "of the Devil" and one of the seven deadly sins. Yes, anger is devilish when inappropriately expressed. But anger expressed properly is a God-given blessing that, as you will see, increases your energy, self-worth, peace of mind, and closeness to your self and your loved ones.

When felt and expressed appropriately, anger leads to a feeling of release, to a deep guttural sigh—"Ahhh!"—that means "I feel better. I finally got that off my chest." This feeling is hard to represent in print because "Ahhh!" looks like what we say when the doctor inspects our tonsils. But that's the feeling we want to get to: a huge release of breath, of tension, of anxiety, of frustration.

Are you conscious of how you breathe? Please try to be. As you read this book, you're going to remember many times when you've been angry or sad or both. Notice how your breathing changes—notice how your body changes in posture and tension—as you live in your feelings.

Now, breathe in. Breathe out. Breathe *way* in. And as you breathe out, say "Ahhh!" Make that "Ahhh!" loud and deep.

When I write "Ahhh!" hereafter, you know that's the feeling and sound I mean.

WHAT MAKES YOU ANGRY?

Your anger is your response to the world not going as you wish. You feel anger when you hit your thumb with a hammer. Your car breaks down a week after the warranty expired. Your parents don't come through with a loan. Your son leaves shaving cream on the mirror. Your unmarried daughter gets pregnant. Someone cuts you off on the highway. The referee makes a bad call. The price of gasoline jumps ten cents. A colleague in your office gets mugged. An air-traffic controller's mistake causes a crash. Kids keep starting to smoke. No compromise is found in Northern Ireland or the Middle East. War breaks out. Children suffer. People starve. People starve other people.

The world makes you furious, it's so wrong. Unjust. Stupid. Unfair. The world is full of things to be angry at, always has been, always will be. (And one day we, and everyone we care about, will die. That strikes me as exasperating, to put it mildly.) We get angry to protest the unfairness of life and the shabby way we're treated.

Occasionally—*very* rarely—our anger produces results. As infants, we awakened at night and howled, and our fury may have brought a parent (if we had good parents) from the dark to pick us up, hold us, warm us, dry us, give us food. If no parent came, we continued to cry, but in twenty minutes—eternity to an infant—our tears would turn from rage and anger to hurt and grief at the way the world was, and then to helplessness and hopelessness. We had been exposed to the lesson life endlessly teaches: protest may do no good; the only recourse may be mourning.

Anger is caused by frustration over the fact that the world is not made to satisfy our desires. Anger is thus inescapable, with us in the cradle and with us as we face our death. If we are human, we get angry. Even Jesus and Gandhi got angry.

ISN'T ANGER UNHEALTHY?

No. And yes.

Anger expressed—pushed out from the body—is as healthy as any other emotion.

Anger repressed, anger suppressed, anger inhibited, anger kept in the body is toxic.

Doctors are just beginning to understand how dangerous internalized anger is. Medical researchers have found that people who suppress their anger, people given to suspiciousness, fuming, and recurrent hostile rages, are putting their lives at risk as much as people who smoke and people who are grossly overweight.

Dr. Mara Julius, an epidemiologist at the University of Michigan, ran personality tests on a large group of women in 1971. Nineteen years later she reinterviewed those women who were still alive. She found that the women who in 1971 had showed signs of "chronic anger" and "long-term suppressed anger" were three times as likely to have died as other women their age.

The crucial difference among the women in Dr. Julius's experiment was not that some of them felt anger and the others didn't. *All* of them felt anger, but some expressed the anger, and others suppressed it. Many of the suppressors paid with their lives.

A study published in the *American Journal of Cardiology* (August, 1992) found that when people with heart disease reconstruct incidents that still make them angry, the pumping efficiency of their heart drops by five percentage points. This is a temporary, but significant, impairment and demonstrates a direct link to anger and heart function. Earlier studies have shown that people who are by nature more hostile and irritable are as much as five times more likely to die at an early age from heart disease. Dr. Gail Ironson, a psychiatrist at the University of Miami and lead researcher on the study, says that the healthiest way to handle anger is to "express it with assertiveness, telling those involved that you're upset and why, but not in an angry way."

Other medical studies, cited by psychologist James Pennebaker in his *Opening Up: The Healing Power of Confiding in Others* (1990), link repressed anger to elevated cholesterol levels, high blood pressure, hypertension, heart attacks and other cardiovascular problems, immune system disorders including white-blood-cell count abnormalities, breast cancer, asthma, diabetes, anorexia nervosa, and greater susceptibility to pain, as well as to everyday complaints like headaches, stomachaches, and backaches.

Suppressing our anger,

repressing it,
internalizing it,
turning it back on ourselves,
swallowing it,
storing it within us,
inhibiting it,
burying it,
"eating it,"
"stuffing it,"

can have catastrophic results for our health.

Furthermore, the very act of holding anger in itself takes energy— which is unhealthy because it leaves us less energy for everything positive in our lives. So when we hold in anger, we're tired most of the time. We fall prey to infection. We have problems performing sexually.

Finally, to numb the anger that is chained inside us, we are likely to be driven to addiction: to alcohol, drugs, food, work, TV, sex, sleep, or compulsive behavior.

Suppressed anger is harmful. Over two, ten, thirty years, it can kill.

Anger expressed appropriately, on the other hand, can actually keep us healthy. If you follow my suggestions for getting anger out of your body, I believe you will find your physical health improves. You'll sleep better. You'll have fewer stomach problems and migraines, reduced chance of heart disease, a stronger immune system and thus less likelihood of cancer and infection, more energy, and more intense sexual release because you're more in touch with your body.

Healthier yourself, you'll also have healthier relations with other people. You'll stand up for your rights and appropriate boundaries, and you'll defend yourself against other people's efforts to control you. At the same time, you won't be expecting them to fix the defects in your life. You'll give up trying to control them with rages or manipulation.

The bottom line for me is that feeling anger and expressing it properly makes a person happier. I've seen this occur in my life and with hundreds of other people. When you begin getting the anger out of your body, your darkness and brooding start to lift. Your brow unfurrows. Your voice loses its edge of pleading and harshness. Your medical problems diminish. Your body gets looser, more supple. You laugh more often and more deeply. Your body, your personality, your whole being is lighter. Your spirit is freer.

You become, quite simply, more authentic, more *actualized,* more yourself. And more content being yourself.

Sounds good, eh? It is.

But it takes us a while and some work to get there.

1
The Child's Equation: Anger Equals Pain and Abandonment

The chief thing that keeps us from feeling and experiencing anger is fear. Given what happened to most of us in childhood, our fears are understandable.

Most of us grew up in homes where, when someone got angry, someone got hurt. When my dad got angry, I got whipped, rejected, ridiculed, sent to my room. When my mom got angry, she withdrew, shut up, went away, sent me away. When I got angry, I got hit, rejected, ridiculed, deprived of dinner, sent to my room till I could come out "in a better mood."

So, like most of us, I learned while I was young the anger-pain equation: If someone gets angry, someone gets hurt.

I learned this equation before I was five, but I didn't learn it in a *conscious* way. It was something my body knew long before my mind could put it into words.

My body knew it because it knew what I was feeling. My body does my feeling for me. Your body does your feeling for you. Every feeling—from pleasure to pain and everything between—we feel in our bodies first and only secondarily through our minds.

When I was a young child, my body learned that anger brought on pain, and it instinctively found a way of protecting me against pain. It had me avoid anger.

"If Dad's angry, run away," my body told me.

"If Mom's angry, nod and say you're sorry. Try to do something nice for her. Then run away."

And if I was angry?

Stop it! Hide it. Deny it. Swallow it and count to ten. Count to a hundred. Pray. Be ashamed. Run away.

The boy in me flew away from feeling sad and angry and became a Flying Boy man who flies away not only from his own feelings but from anybody who wants him to feel.

MY BODY MAY HAVE SAVED MY LIFE WHEN I WAS YOUNG

I happened to be born into a family so dysfunctional that if my body hadn't known to avoid anger, I might not have survived.

Even if this was not true for you, you are likely also to have internalized the anger-pain equation and the lesson of avoiding anger. If you know that when someone is angry someone else is going to get hurt—emotionally, physically, psychologically, spiritually—the only healthy thing to do is avoid anger at all costs.

As children we had to avoid anger to protect ourselves. As adults we still have to protect ourselves against *unsafe* anger—which means anger that intends to hurt us or someone else. This is a point I'll emphasize later on.

By the end of this book, though, I am going to suggest a revision of the anger-pain equation we learned as children. I am going to suggest that in all cases involving safe and mature adults, the equation is false and harmful. The new equation I'm going to suggest is *anger, when felt and expressed appropriately, equals energy, intimacy, and serenity.*

Now, if you're like most people reading this book, you probably don't believe this. You're in good company: Most mental health therapists don't believe it, either. Simply reading this book won't make a believer of you. You will have to test the truth or falsity of my equation in your own life, in safe circumstances, little by little over time. You will have to see whether, when you are angry and feel and express your anger in ways I will explain, you feel better, without having hurt yourself or others.

THE LEGACY OF CHILDHOOD

As I've suggested, the way we deal with anger—and most other emotions—originates in our childhood. If we can't express our anger now, and many of us don't dare to, this is because our parents or whoever occupied the place of parents for us didn't accept our anger when we were young. If we express our anger now in inappropriate ways, ways that hurt us or other people, we learned to do this from our parents.

Our parents expressed their nonacceptance of us and our anger in many ways. They punished our bodies with hits and withholding of food. They criticized, shamed, and ridiculed us. They withheld affection, were absent from us, sent us away. They ignored us, gave us the silent treatment, even flatly denied they knew us.

The last punishment was used by Jill Ker Conway's parents when she was growing up on a remote farm, Coorain, in Australia. Conway tells about the punishment and its consequences in her 1989 autobiography, *The Road from Coorain*. When she misbehaved as a child, she says,

> my parents simply acted as though I were not their child but a stranger. They would inquire civilly as to who I was and what I was doing on Coorain, but no hint of recognition escaped them. This treatment never failed to reduce me to abject contrition. In later life my recurring nightmares were always about my inability to prove to people I knew quite

well who I was. I became an unnaturally good child, and accepted uncritically that goodness was required of me if my
parents' disappointments in life were ever to be compensated
for.

Conway, a historian and the former president of Smith College, writes
of her suffering in a reserved way, but she still makes us know how
much it hurt and haunts her.

The truth is that nearly all of us are haunted by the treatment we
received as infants and children. When we are children, our parents
seem to be gods to us. For those endless first years, until we are five
or eight or even ten or more, whatever our parents do must be right.
If they hit us or mock us or ignore us, we must deserve it. We must
be somehow defective.

As young children, we *must* have our parents' acceptance. We will
do literally anything, submit to any abuse, however painful to ourselves, not to be abandoned by them. And every punishment they
give us then—whipping, criticism, withholding, absence, silence—
is a form of abandonment.

If we're afraid to be angry now, if we're afraid to be ourselves
and spontaneously feel and express whatever we want—grief, love,
pleasure, need, joy—it's because we couldn't be ourselves then. We
couldn't be ourselves then because we feared abandonment. When
we can't be ourselves now, it's for the same reason.

Above all, if we can't express our anger with people now, it's
because we couldn't express our anger with our parents then. Because
we feared they would leave us.

UNTIL WE CONQUER OUR FEAR OF ABANDONMENT...

... we're going to be afraid to be ourselves.

Afraid of asserting ourselves. Of insisting on our rights. Of protecting our boundaries. Of getting angry.

We'll be afraid to say what we really feel or to do what we really want, lest people think us crazy, immoral, lazy, selfish, overemo- tional, underemotional, or disgusting.

And abandon us.

So we do like the young Jill Conway. We act unnaturally—that is, against our nature. We are "unnaturally good," diligent, obedient, cheerful, thrifty, brave, clean, reverent, and the rest of the Scout litany. We break our backs to be pretty enough, smart enough, funny enough, rich enough, inexpensive enough, indispensable enough, that we won't be left.

Or if we were taught as children that we were hopelessly bad, worthless no matter what we did, we probably behave "unnaturally" in the opposite direction. We're criminals, sociopaths, rapists, sadists, child molesters, killers. We recapitulate the relation we had with our parents, and the relationship they had with their parents, by making sure we'll be abandoned by *everyone*—always, I think, with the unspoken, unkillable belief in us that, despite all, we will somehow be loved, forgiven, totally accepted, as we weren't as children.

ARE YOU AN ABANDONMENT ADDICT?

The sociopaths among us reflect the important but unrecognized fact that abandonment can be addictive.

As children, we couldn't stand to be abandoned because, at bottom, we realized we couldn't survive alone. Yet we *were* abandoned. All of us were, I believe—even those of us who think we weren't. And we were abandoned by our parents, people we loved more than we'll ever love anyone.

So abandonment came to feel not only right to us and what we deserved, but *like love*.

How many of us are victims of the mistaken belief that abuse means affection? You hear it all the time. "He really loves me, he treats me so mean." "I'm crazy about her—she's one tough woman."

We become accustomed to people not being there for us to the point that we feel that it is *right*. Leaving looks like loving. We become addicted to being abandoned as we become addicted to alcohol, coffee, or cigarettes. Alcohol, caffeine, and nicotine are bad, but if you have them every day and then stop, you miss them. You *crave* them. You're uncomfortable without them.

Nine out of ten times, those of us who had a cold mother or distant father choose a cold wife or distant husband. Because that's what love feels like to us: no love. Many of us *can't* fall in love with someone who is *not* like one or both of our parents. At least we can't do it until we've recovered from our childhood. And finally grown up. (The Chinese have a saying: "The first wife is for your parents; the second is for you.") We can't do it until we've gotten over, or mostly over, our fear of abandonment.

Because we're addicted to the patterns of our childhood, we set ourselves up to be abandoned, and if someone *doesn't* abandon us, we often abandon ourselves. That's what the sociopath does, and the depressive, and the self-pitier, like the thirty-year-old man who can't bathe or shave or sleep or eat because his love has left him and he's become a three-year-old again, incapable of caring for himself, weeping and moping; or like the sixty-year-old woman whose husband has died and who comforts herself with months of chocolate cake and gin.

BREAKING THE CYCLE OF ABANDONMENT

The only way we can overcome our feeling of abandonment is to *feel* it. Grieve it. Rage over it. Express it with the body and *from* the body. In tears and shouts and groans and sobs.

Until we do this, we will be condemned to:

• not be ourselves, hoping thereby to avoid abandonment
• bury our real feelings, swallow our anger, ignore our rights, renounce our power
• people-please, be "unnaturally good," do whatever is

necessary to keep from reexperiencing abandonment in the
form of someone leaving us
• make our spouse, lover, parent, child, boss, mentor, or priest
  our be-all and end-all, our God, our Higher Power, our reason
  for living, for whom we will do anything, say anything, and
  be any way, and from whom we will take anything
• be dependent
• abandon ourselves
• be angry—for all the reasons given above

How do we experience and express our feelings of abandonment?
One way is to do the emotional-release exercises of the sort I'm
going to describe later on for anger and grief. (But right now, you
can be aware of your breathing. Did it change as you read the above
list? Did you "catch your breath"—that is, *stop* breathing? Keep
breathing. Take a deep breath, in and out. Again, in and out. You
can decrease fear and anxiety when you breathe consciously.) Such
exercises work for abandonment, too, because abandonment is the
deepest of our buried emotional hurts. Indeed, when you do work
on your anger and grief, you're also working on your feelings of
abandonment and vice versa. But you can't get to the bottom levels
of your anger and grief until you consciously recognize and feel your
abandonment.

To be motivated to do this and to feel safe doing it, you need to
be persuaded of two crucial facts:

1. You have been abandoned.
2. Adults can't be abandoned, except by themselves.

YOU HAVE BEEN ABANDONED

Even if you think you weren't.

You were abandoned as a child. I'm willing to bet on it.

A great many people deny this by saying their parents didn't spank them or threaten them, never raised their voices, didn't criticize, never withheld affection, and never left them.

But the harder people assure me they weren't abandoned, the more I am sure they were. Denial saves them from having to go through the grief and rage that always follow embracing the truth. Denial protects them from losing their idealized childhood and mourning the self they didn't become, and from having to hate their parents and then learn to love them in a new, sadder, but authentic and adult way.

I remember one man, a client who had spent a decade going through lovers at a six- to ten-a-year rate. He was positive he hadn't been abandoned.

"How about your trouble settling down with a woman?" I said.

"That has absolutely nothing to do with my parents," he said. He'd worked his way through college waiting tables in a fraternity, where he'd seen an endless parade of gorgeous young women at parties and felt too poor and ugly to approach them. "Once I had the money," he said (he was a lawyer), "I started taking revenge— you know, by making it with all these different women."

"So now you're happy with your life," I said.

"John, come on!" he said. "Of course I'm not. That's why I'm seeing you."

"If you're not happy with your life," I said, "then you were abandoned as a child. If you'd been made to feel totally okay as a child, you would feel okay about your life today. When you saw a girl you liked in the fraternity house, you would have approached her. If she turned you down, you would still have been okay. You would have said to yourself, 'I'm okay. I don't need her. With or without her, I'm a fine person.' That's what you'd say to yourself now, too: 'Married or single, I'm a fine person. I'm the best possible me.' "

If our parents didn't instill a sense of well-being in us, if they didn't support our being who we really were, they abandoned us. It takes a lot of work, self-sacrifice, love, and *time* to instill real self-worth in an infant and a young child. And it is done best in traditional societies, where parents and clan members live in constant closeness with children.

The childrearing pattern of such societies is examined in Jean Liedloff's extraordinary book, *The Continuum Concept* (1975, 1986), which I recommend to any parent with a young child or anybody intending to become a parent. Liedloff, who lived with the Yequana, a tribe in the Venezuelan jungle, argues that modern society's method of childrearing goes against the way infants and young children have been raised since the dawn of our species. She suggests that infants up to the age of eighteen months or two years or until they have such trust of the world that they are content to explore it on their own, should be at all times, sleeping and waking, in the company of a parent or other caregiver who provides as much "in-arms" comfort and carrying, and food, play, attention, and affection as the child wants.

Liedloff romanticizes tribal life and does nothing to prove her claim that the childrearing pattern she found among the Yequana is common to primitive cultures the world over. Nonetheless, the ideal she saw there is powerfully appealing, and her ability to view our system of childrearing through an infant's eyes is uncanny. Here, much abridged, is her description of the newborn infant's arrival in one of "the maternity wards of Western civilization":

> The newborn infant is put in a box where he is left, no matter how he weeps, in a limbo that is utterly motionless (for the first time in all his body's experience, during the eons of its evolution or during its eternity of bliss in the womb). The only sounds he can hear are the wails of other victims of the same ineffable agony. The sound can mean nothing to him. He cries and cries; his lungs, new to air, are strained with the desperation in his heart. No one comes. Trusting in the rightness of life, as by nature he must, he does the only act he can, which is to cry on. Eventually, a timeless lifetime later, he falls asleep exhausted.
>
> He awakes in a mindless terror at the silence, the motionlessness. He screams. He is afire from head to foot with

want, with desire, with intolerable impatience. He gasps for breath and screams until his head is filled and throbbing with the sound. He screams until his chest aches, until his throat is sore. He can bear the pain no more and his sobs weaken and subside. He listens. He opens and closes his fists. He rolls his head from side to side. Nothing helps. It is unbearable. He begins to cry again, but it is too much for his strained throat; he soon stops. He stiffens his desire-racked body and there is a shadow of relief. He waves his hands and kicks his feet. He stops, able to suffer, unable to think, unable to hope. He listens. Then he falls asleep again.

Someone comes and lifts him deliciously through the air. He is in life. He is carried a bit too gingerly for his taste, but there is motion. He rests in the enfolding arms, and though his skin is sending no message of relief from the cloth, no news of live flesh on his flesh, his hands and mouth are re-porting normal. The positive pleasure of life, which is contin-uum normal, is almost complete. The taste and texture of the breast are there, the warm milk is flowing into his eager mouth, there is a heartbeat, which should have been his reas-surance of continuity from the womb, there is movement per-ceptible to his dim vision. The sound of the voice is right, too. He sucks and, when he feels full and rosy, dozes off.

When he awakens he is in hell. No memory, no hope, no thought can bring the comfort of his visit to his mother into this bleak purgatory. Hours pass and days and nights. He screams, tires, sleeps.

By the time he is taken to his mother's home (surely it cannot be called his) he is well versed in the character of life. On a preconscious plane that will qualify all his further impressions, he knows life to be unspeakably lonely, unrespon-sive to his signals, and full of pain.

Do you say you weren't abandoned?

If Liedloff's description of infant deprivation moved you—made you mad, made you sad—you were abandoned. The Yequana wouldn't understand what she was talking about. As Liedloff says, it would be literally incredible to them that children are treated this way.

(I have to tell you that reading Liedloff's passage made me so furious I had to do some of the anger-release exercises I'll be explaining to you; I screamed into a pillow and, later, pounded the daylights out of a racquetball for fifteen minutes. Even then, I couldn't bring myself to write anything more that day.)

Is it possible there are still people like the Yequana—people who have no sense of estrangement from the roots of their being—people *un*abandoned?

Frankly, I doubt it, but I hope someday to go and find out for myself.

The behaviorist psychologist B. F. Skinner believed such people could be produced in the modern world if we devised the proper, positively responsive childhood environment. He said that the children of this environment, when they came to read Dostoyevski's novels at age eighteen, wouldn't understand what he was talking about.

It's not going to happen soon. My own feeling is that it will never, *can* never happen, for two reasons.

The first, more trivial reason is that abandonment can happen quickly and *easily*, without anyone intending it. Up to this point, I've spoken of abandonment as though all of it is like beating, ridicule, and withholding love and attention—that is, consciously malicious. This is not at all the case.

A six-month-old is crying in his crib, and his mother can't come—she's in the shower, say, or on the phone long distance. She glances at the baby and sees he's okay. Just crying and wanting to be picked up. She goes ahead and gets dressed or keeps talking. Twenty minutes whiz past before she gets him.

That twenty minutes may be all it takes for that particular baby. It seems like forever to him. He feels he's been abandoned, he's not cared for. So at age forty, when a girlfriend leaves or a boss reneges on a promise, there's a six-month-old infant howling in a man who can't say why he's so angry or why he's crying from such depths.

Can one incident of abandonment during infancy really have so much impact? We'd like to think not. We'd like to think it requires a *lot* of abandonment—or as a social worker might say, "a strong pattern of dysfunctional behavior." But who can say for certain? One thing we do know: The millions of men and women who are afraid of being abandoned didn't *start* being afraid in their adulthood. I was at the airport the other day and heard a young father tell his rambunctious toddler son, "If you don't settle down and behave, I'm going to leave you here." Later, the father got so annoyed that he actually started walking down the hall. Can you assure me that that incident didn't have an effect on the boy? He screamed as if it might have.

Separation, loss, abandonment potentially happen anytime a parent leaves the room. I don't see how, given our socioeconomic system, we can avoid it. (B. F. Skinner went through a period of thinking it might be avoided by raising babies in temperature-controlled rubber boxes. Lots of luck.) Even if we could rework our system to avoid it, I'm pretty sure we wouldn't.

And even if we *could* eliminate unintentional, situational abandonment, we can't fix the second and more important reason why abandonment is unavoidable. Abandonment is unavoidable because of the way we are and the way life is. We are human and thus self-aware and thus conscious that we are individuals and alone and separated from the power that put us in the world. We know we can't control the most important aspects of our existence—can't prolong summer, can't change what we did in the past, can't bring back the dead.

We know—and many of us feel this every day as a huge hollowness at our center—that life is a continual *losing* of people, moments, and events that will never again be exactly as they were.

ADULTS CAN'T BE ABANDONED

If you're over fifteen, you can't be abandoned.

You may *feel* abandoned, but that's the needy child in you, longing for someone else to approve, accept, admire, validate, sponsor, and take responsibility for you. Make it better, Daddy. Kiss it, Mommy, and make it go away.

Adults can't be abandoned because we can take care of ourselves. As adults, if our spouse of twenty-seven years leaves, if we're fired from our job, we have resources: friends and acquaintances and services to call upon. We have our car keys and checkbooks and credit cards. We know how to take care of ourselves and our needs so that we feel good again—or if we don't know, we're learning or we need to learn.

We know, or we're learning, that we can't count on our spouse or lover or child or parent or friend or Significant Other to make us not feel abandoned. We've tried to put this burden on people, and they've always let us down. When they've tried to be all we needed them to be—and they did try, some of them—they finally got angry at us for what we were demanding. To our surprise, we got angry at them not only for failing to come through but, often, for giving in to our demands and *trying* to come through.

We know, or we are learning, that we can only count on ourselves to make us feel unabandoned. We know we need support, hugs, positive reinforcement, a healthy diet, meaningful work, intellectual enrichment, spiritual expression, sexual release, and enough rest and recreation, and we know to take responsibility for getting them.

The only way we adults can be abandoned is to do it to ourselves and say, for instance, "I can't be happy unless I have him," or "her," or "their approval," or "your forgiveness," or "Mom and Dad's blessing," or "a sports car," or "a vice-presidency in a Fortune 500 company," or "a million dollars." Statements like these show an infantile longing to control other people and things and make them the basis of *our* life, our reason for being, our God. Such statements show that the speaker hasn't dealt with his or her childhood abandonment.

When we *have* dealt with our abandonment, we know how to be our own best friend. How to let go of others and mind our own damned business. How to stand up for ourself. How—if our name is Joan Doe (or John Smith)—to be the best Joan Doe (or John Smith) we can be.

Theodore Roosevelt liked to tell people he made decisions by asking himself, "What would Lincoln do?" I sometimes ask myself "What would John Lee do?" because, at my strongest, I'm the best John Lee ever.

When we have dealt with our feelings of abandonment, we know how to take care of ourselves forevermore. If we speak our truth and other people can't handle it and leave us, we will be hurt and sad and angry that they left, but we'll be very much okay.

2
The Unsafe Angers and Our Escapes

As children, we feared anger because, in our experience, it caused pain and abandonment. It hurt us because it *meant* to hurt us. It was unsafe anger, like my father's rage or my mother's passive aggression or my own self-directed anger.

Whether we are children or adults, we are right to fear the unsafe angers and we are right to avoid them or defend ourselves against them.

UNSAFE ANGERS

Rage

The most obvious and shocking form of unsafe anger is rage. Rage explodes outward, into the world, from the person who is angry. An accountant is cut off on the highway and chases the offending car, blowing her horn. An employee fired by a post office comes back the next day with a rifle and kills two of his bosses, a secretary, and five people he never saw before. A mother finds her lost child in the mall and shrieks at the boy and hits him.

Rage is the most violent human emotion. To direct it toward a person—some would say toward any living thing—is uncivilized and contemptible, except when our survival is at stake.

Rage is anger uncontrolled because it is uncontrollable. Rage literally cannot be contained in the body. As we'll see later on, rage is anger that has been buried and accumulating for years, often since childhood, that suddenly erupts when it is triggered by its resemblance to a present-day event or situation. Rage usually scares the person who feels and expresses it, though often not *at the moment* of expression. Rage always scares everybody else in the vicinity.

Passive Aggression

Not all unsafe anger directed outward toward the world is explosive. The anger that psychologists call passive aggression is subtle rage. It also goes out from an angry person into the world, but instead of exploding, it *sneaks* out. Whereas rage is artillery openly fired at the enemy, passive aggression is a guerrilla patrol carrying knives to cut him down before he realizes there is an enemy around.

Once I lived with a woman I didn't want to live with anymore. I was too nice a guy to tell her the truth, so I let my feelings toward her ooze out sideways. I made fun of her taste in music, movies, books, and former lovers. I called her (she was a short woman) an intellectual bonsai. When she made a salad dressing that smelled strong, I said it tasted like athlete's foot powder. I had seen my father hit my mother, and I was proud that I had never hit a woman. I didn't need to. I could cut a woman to pieces with my tongue.

In the long run, anger that means to hurt other people—even if it's quiet, passive, sideways anger—is unhealthy to relationships.

Implosive Anger

Implosive anger is rage directed inward.

It is significant that whereas we have lots of terms for outward-directed anger (rage, fury, wrath, tantrum, outburst, fit), we have none for anger that's directed inward.

Yet when I ask people in my workshops who they are *most* angry at, nine times out of ten the answer is "myself."

I think self-directed anger is generally more damaging than the other unsafe angers. It can be propelled by the bitterest rage, but all its force remains in the body of its author. It can act like a grenade that a soldier pulls the pin on and clasps to his heart.

It's easy to see how this anger can lead to suicide and stroke and migraine and depression and self-hatred and self-pity. In my case, it led to such depression and self-hatred that I became an eight-year-old religious fanatic and a sixteen-year-old nicotine fiend and alcoholic.

WAYS OF "ESCAPING" ANGER

Because the anger we experienced as children led to pain for us and others, we learned to run away from it. This was both necessary and tragic.

It was necessary because running away offered us some protection, and as I've said, whether we are children or adults, we must always protect ourselves against anger that means to hurt us.

It was tragic for two reasons. First, we protected ourselves by attempting to "escape" anger, which isn't possible and which in fact buried the anger more deeply in us. Second, we ran away not only from unsafe anger but from *all* anger. We set up a pattern of anger-avoidance that has devastating consequences for our mental and physical health.

The following are the escapes we learned as children and that most of us use throughout our lives.

Shutting Down

In the earliest escape, our body, hurt or threatened with hurt, shuts down.

This response is instinctive. It is built into the most primitive part of our brain, the part we get from our reptilian ancestors. The response protects us from feeling too much by numbing us out. Thanks to this response, after the first dozen hits with a paddle, our body hardly feels the rest.

The shutdown response is triggered by fear of hurt as well as by actual hurt. How? Look at the way you and I react when we receive an injection. Or look at how we respond to a horror movie when we know the psychopath is waiting in the closet with a hatchet. We hold our breath, get tense, turn off. Maybe we close our eyes or duck our heads. Maybe we say, "Is it over yet?"—*it* being the threat to our feelings.

Most of us come out of childhood reacting to anger by shutting down. We freeze like rabbits in the headlights of an oncoming car. When anger is around, we feel it in our bodies so strongly that we make our emotions as dead as we can.

Let me tell you about Tom, a forty-three-year-old man in a men's support group I led. Tom was *big* and quiet and hostile—one of those men who look as if nothing fazes them. He had mastered that look because he was terrified of his own anger. He had seen what a big man's anger could do to a room and the people in it when he was a boy and his father went into his Friday- and Saturday-night rages. As a grown man, Tom wore an expression that sneered, "Don't mess with me because you don't dare to see me angry"—which was unnecessary, because even when something got him angry, he didn't show it. He shut down, just as he had as a kid.

Tom's wife was frightened of his bottled-up emotions and annoyed by them at the same time. Whenever things got stormy between them, he would disappear into himself, and she would have no one to fight with. After fifteen years of marriage, she left.

A couple of years later, after months of attending our men's group, Tom finally felt his anger. It was an awesome but totally safe explosion of rage, pain, and tears. Tom did half a dozen sessions of emotional-release work, and his face grew a lot less frozen and mean. Today, the woman he's with has a partner who gets angry and who openly *and safely* feels and expresses his anger.

As I said, we shut down our bodies instinctively at first. Our response precedes our conscious will. Once we see how effectively shutting down protects us, though, we *learn* to do it. Our bodily reflex becomes the basis of the most common escape from anger we use thereafter.

The Intellectual Escape (Or, Going Up into Our Heads)

As very young children, perhaps as young as four or five, we learned to "control" our own anger and protect ourselves from other people's anger by going up into our heads and either commanding our bodies to shut down or rationalizing away the anger directed at us.

Expressions of anger by us or by other people led to our bodies being cuffed, hit, whipped, ridiculed, shamed, sent away, and deprived of food, hugs, and approval. We thus learned that our bodies were bad or not good enough, certainly not safe places to be. We found that the quickest defense was to turn ourselves off from the neck down, freeze our feelings, and escape into our heads, so that no matter what was done to our bodies or said about them, we wouldn't feel it.

Has anyone ever said to you, "Why don't you say anything? Why do you just sit there and let me attack you?"

If so, it suggests that the strategy you used as a child to defend yourself from your parents' anger was to escape into your head. Shutting down your body then said to your parents what it says now to people who are angry at you: "Go on. Say or do whatever you like. I'm not here."

As children, we used our minds not only to freeze our feelings but to rationalize away the wrongs our parents did us. We had to do this to survive. As I've said, until we are five or eight or ten or more, we feel that whatever our parents do must be right. If they hit us or mock us or ignore us or even incest us, we feel we deserve it. We must be somehow defective.

Say your father screamed at you and slapped you when he was drunk, or your mother failed to pick you up after the movies because she was weeping too much to get out of bed. You would go into your head to find reasons to numb down the hurt.

"I must have been doing something wrong," you'd tell yourself.

Or later: "He was drunk. He notices everything I do wrong when he's drunk."

Or still later: "She was sick. I know I'm not supposed to do anything to annoy her when she's sick."

The child always assumes that he or she is wrong and the parent is right.

The intellectual escape is our first conscious refuge from anger. It is also the "answer to anger" offered in such books as *Anger: The Misunderstood Emotion, The Dance of Anger,* and *Of Course You're Angry.* These books argue that the way to deal with our anger is to go up into our heads and "understand" it. They say that if we acknowledge that we are angry and then seek out the reasons for our anger, we will have dealt with it. They quote with approval psychologist William James's advice: "Refuse to express a passion, and it dies. Count to ten before venting your anger, and its occasion seems ridiculous."

I totally disagree.

James's advice assumes that human beings are primarily creatures of reason, intellect, and spirit. It suggests that our minds are always dominant—and they are not. We are a mindbody (or bodymind). As much as we are mental beings, we are also physical, animal, visceral, and biological. Part angel, part ape.

And anger isn't primarily mental. Anger is a *physical* energy housed in the body—as the other emotions are. Anger isn't linear or logical or rational or justifiable or reasonable. Anger just is. Like love. Hunger. Apathy. Joy.

The advice William James gives could as well be applied to any other emotion, but see how odd it would sound:

"You're experiencing joy now—but stop! Refuse to express the passion. Instead, think about it. Think about where it's coming from, and it will go away. You'll be indifferent to the beautiful breeze, the thought of your lover's body, or your child's laughter."

Would *thinking* about these things reduce their sweetness? If you continued the thinking process long and hard enough, for ten minutes, say, the emotion might dissipate. You might come to say, as William James did, "Okay, I thought about my anger for ten minutes, and I'm not feeling it anymore. So I must not be angry."

I believe you'd be wrong. You would have used your mind to stuff your anger down into your body. And your body would now have to get rid of the anger somehow, at a later time.

You say you've thought about your anger and made it go away. Then two hours later somebody cuts you off on the highway, and you want to take your lug wrench and beat his head in. Or the dog jumps up on your suit, and you scream at it and give it a vicious kick. Your actions show your anger hasn't gone. Using your reason to suppress the anger left you prey to such "reasonable" impulses as wanting to kill someone on the highway and kicking your dog.

The intellectual escape is much advocated, but by itself it doesn't work.

The Spiritual Escape

The spiritual escape, which I prefer to call the spiritual bypass, is like the intellectual escape, except that religion replaces reason. You "bypass" anger by praying, meditating, chanting, and focusing your attention on higher things.

For more than five years in my late twenties and early thirties, I used the techniques of Eastern meditation, trying to overcome my anger and pain. When things were particularly bad, I'd be meditating two and three hours a day.

I remember once when my girlfriend and I were having a fight, I came out from several hours of meditating in the bedroom, and she said, "Still angry, eh?" She was looking at how tense I was and at how gently I was moving so as not to shake the calm I'd managed to induce.

"I'm not angry," I said. "I don't get angry. I told you that."

"John, you're shouting," she said.

"Shit!" I said. "Thanks a lot! Now I'll have to meditate some more."

There is nothing more important to me than our human relation to a power higher than us. But this Higher Power is no better than our human intellect at taking care of the emotions that dwell in our bodies.

Feelings are meant to be felt, not prayed away. Spiritual practices are meant to enhance our connection to our God, not to remove anger. When they are used on anger, all they do is push the anger down into the body, where it becomes an impediment to spiritual life.

That's why some of the angriest people are also the most religious. They find their god—the God of the Old Testament, say—satisfying because He attacks what they're angry at. "I'm not angry at your loose life," they tell you. "God is. I'm too spiritual to get angry at fornications and blaspheming. But God's angry, and He's going to punish you. He's going to make sure you suffer endless, endless damnation."

I'm sorry to say that one of the strongest advocates of the spiritual escape from anger is Alcoholics Anonymous. I say this as a member of AA and ACoA and Codependents Anonymous.

Bill W., the co-founder of AA, says again and again that if we're disturbed by anger or any other emotion, our first priority has to be to "quiet that disturbance" by turning it over to God as we individually understand God.

If turning it over works for you, fine. But I've tried it, and it doesn't work for me. I've decided that God expects me to take care of my own anger and my other emotions. And I believe that since my emotions are in my body, my body is designed (by God, if you like) to deal with my emotions.

AA wants us to substitute religion for alcohol—the spiritual for spirits. But some AA members use the spiritual for the same purpose that they use alcohol: to deaden their feelings so they won't feel them.

Which brings us to . . .

The Addiction Escape

I have already said the main thing I want to say about addiction. It is an escape from feeling.

We use our addictions—alcohol, drugs, cigarettes, food, work, TV, caffeine, sex, sleep, pornography, compulsive thoughts and behavior—to numb us against feeling.

We awaken in the morning a bit out of sorts, but rather than examine what's going on inside us and digging down through the crust of our emotions into what's underneath, we reach for a cigarette, a cup of coffee, and a big sweet roll. We bury that out-of-sorts feeling with the artificial energy of our addiction. When the energy wears off in an hour or two, we feel let down. That out-of-sorts feeling, which we haven't expressed and so haven't gotten rid of, is still gnawing at us. We drink more coffee and eat a chocolate bar. We fight the out-of-sorts feeling all day, maybe for several days. Maybe for weeks. (Addiction not only deadens our feelings but makes them last much, much longer.)

Medical researchers have recently suggested that addiction to cigarettes and coffee is the way a great many people cope with unrecognized and undiagnosed depression. People medicate themselves with the drugs caffeine and nicotine throughout the day to ward off their feelings of emptiness. In doing this, they are quite like *illegal* drug users, most of whom are also escaping feelings they don't want to face.

All addictions work toward the same goal: to dissociate mind from body, thinking from feeling. Praying your anger away is like watching six hours of TV is like having four beers is like writing a hundred-item list on why you're a very lucky person is like compulsive shopping is like smoking a couple of joints is like sleeping twelve hours a day is like masturbating three times in an evening is like eating a whole cheesecake.

When you give yourself over to your addiction, you're not there anymore. You have abandoned yourself.

What I've said so far about addictions—that they keep us from feeling—is clear and simple. Now things get more complicated.

Most addictions have a numbing or depressant effect. But some do not. Some drugs, legal and illegal, are stimulants. Some drugs, legal and illegal, are stimulants that depress later (alcohol belongs to this group). Some stimulants cause some people to react in ways that make them look as if they are in touch with their feelings. The crack addict rages. The alcoholic rages or gets sentimental. These addicts are expressing feelings—but they are not expressing their true feelings. As I've said, their addictions keep them from their true feelings.

The crack addict or alcoholic shouting his resentments is a helpless, out-of-control victim of a confused jumble of grievances against the world and of unfocused emotions, old and new. The proof that he is not in touch with his real feelings is that the emotions he expresses have no therapeutic effect. He experiences no "Ahhh! I feel better" moment. He heaves no great sigh of release at having gotten the feeling out. He doesn't feel better, and neither do the people around him. They've seen all this before, and they feel cheated, victimized, and exhausted. The next day the addict is back to square one, adrift in the same maelstrom as the day before. He feels as bad as he did before his explosion of emotion. He may actually feel worse because he remembers some of his behavior and is ashamed.

Whether his addiction stimulates or depresses him, the addict gets no "Ahhh!" release because he hasn't *consciously* confronted what he is feeling. Dealing with anger successfully means enlisting both halves of our bodymind, and chemical addiction renders the mind incompetent.

Thus, addiction, whether it stimulates or depresses us, takes from us the necessity, and sometimes the possibility, of feeling whatever is at our core. In fact, addiction takes from us *everything* at our core: joy, ecstasy, excitement, delight, and serenity as well as anger, grief, and pain. Addiction deadens all emotions: those we want, and those we don't.

ALL THESE "ESCAPES" DO THE SAME THING

They deaden anger but don't get it out of our bodies. So rather than freeing us of our anger, they bind us to it.

Fortunately, there is a better way to deal with anger.

3

The Other Angers in Us

Rage, passive aggression, and implosive anger—the "unsafe angers," as I have called them—intend to hurt someone or something. These angers are so frightening that they color our attitude toward *all* anger: We do our best to escape anger because we fear it will cause us pain.

But there are angers besides rage, passive aggression, and implosive anger. In fact, if we define anger as a normal emotional response to life's dissatisfactions, then rage, passive aggression, and implosive anger are not themselves anger but are different ways of manifesting anger. Behind or beneath every rage, say, is a deeply wounded sense of injustice.

Like the other emotions, anger is radically individual and contextual. What makes one person angry may leave another person indifferent. What angers one person at one time in one situation may not have the same effect at another time.

We have different kinds of anger in us and different *depths* of anger on different issues. In our emotional life, each of us is like the earth we live on. We show our feelings—green and sunny, gray and harsh—on the surface, while inside we are honeycombed with different layers of emotion, some near the top, some midlevel, and some so deep as to be, for all we know, bottomless.

To understand the different levels or layers of anger in us, let's develop a scenario in which two people respond differently to the same event.

APPROPRIATE AND INAPPROPRIATE ANGER: TWO SCENARIOS

Ellen works for Edgar in a large bureaucracy. She has spent a long time drafting a report for his signature. She arrives one morning to find the draft on her desk with a note paper-clipped to it:

> Ellen,
>   Thanks very much for the effort. There are some good things here and a lot we'll have to change.
>   See me!
> Edgar

Ellen is annoyed and glares out the window, wondering what she got wrong. She makes an ugly face and mutters a swear word. Then she walks down the hall to the water fountain, has a drink, and brings back a cup of water for the plant on her desk. She sits and thinks, breathing deeply. She phones Edgar's secretary to make an appointment and learns that Edgar's on a skiing vacation and won't be back till the next Tuesday. "Put me down for ten," she says. "And tell him I'm coming to discuss this report I'm doing. I'm concerned that we're working at cross purposes."

Ellen then turns her attention to other work.

Second example. Bob works for Theodore in a bureaucracy and has spent a long time drafting a report for his signature. Bob gets the same note as Ellen, but his response is quite different. He phones Theodore's secretary, Nancy, and on hearing that Theodore's out of town, he blows his stack and asks Nancy how she puts up with such a jerk. He then faxes Theodore a letter saying what he thinks of him (*"Jackass* is too mild a word, and *dumb jackass* is redundant"), how hard he worked on the report ("We're talking weeks, not days—and lots of nights with food brought in"), how thoughtless Theodore was to put him down with such skimpy criticism ("The least you could have done was tell me one thing that's Really Wrong"), and where Theodore can reach him over the weekend.

Ellen and Bob have different responses to a similar situation. Both of them feel anger, but Ellen's is mild and Bob's fierce. Obviously, there could be countless reasons for the difference. For the sake of our thought problem, though, let's make the context of each person's anger as much the same as possible. Let's say that in the past Theodore has praised Bob's work, just as Edgar has praised Ellen's; that Ellen and Bob put in the same amount of time on the project; and that Theodore has told Bob (and Edgar, Ellen) that the report doesn't need to be in final form right away.

In this context, Bob's anger at Theodore's response would seem to most people excessive and inappropriate.

If Bob had been wise, he would have done a "reality check" before blowing up at Nancy and sending that fax. (Later on, I'll talk about reality checks and how we can use them to keep from making mistakes when we express our anger.) Bob didn't check whether his anger was appropriate because, like most of us, he hadn't learned how to take care of his feelings in ways that are safe for him and others.

But again—why is Bob's anger strong and Ellen's mild? The answer to this question can only be found in the two people and their personalities—which means in their histories and the different layers of anger in them.

PRESENT ANGER

Ellen's anger is an example of what I will call *present anger*.

Present anger is caused by present events. It has an emotional force that is appropriate to its cause. It can be expressed in the present moment with little or no anger carried over into the future. Present anger is at the surface of our emotions. Once expressed, it blows away to be replaced by the next top layer of emotion.

Ellen can process her feelings about Edgar and his note without much difficulty. She is annoyed and a bit hurt and puzzled, but her emotions are mild enough that they don't cloud her thinking. She realizes that Edgar may have had new ideas about the report since they last spoke. She knows that even if he didn't like the job she did on this assignment, it's not the end of the world. He generally likes her work. Having thought the matter over, she takes a big breath and lets out a sigh. Now she's ready to know what Edgar's criticisms are and to respond to them. She phones Edgar's secretary and finds that he's gone skiing.

Skiing!

She asks the secretary if Edgar mentioned the report.

No.

Well, if he can go skiing without worrying about the report, Ellen is sure there's no reason she shouldn't relax about it too. In five days she'll talk with him and get his thoughts. The ball's in his court.

She lets out another sigh.

Responding as she has, Ellen expresses all or most of her feelings about the incident. She may have no leftover anger to release later on that day, but if she does, she will get it out in Jazzercise.

SUPPRESSED ANGER

Bob's anger is an example of what I will call *suppressed anger*.

Suppressed anger is anger that is left over from past events. It can be expressed appropriately or inappropriately. Bob expresses his suppressed anger inappropriately. Nearly everybody does. (I'll tell you later how to express your suppressed anger appropriately.)

When a person's response to a present stimulus is inappropriate or excessive, like Bob's response to Theodore's note, we can be fairly sure the present event has revived a past, suppressed anger.

The accountant who blows her horn for a mile alongside a car that cut her off is expressing suppressed anger. Those of us driving behind her know it. We say things like, "She had a bad day at the office." Or, "She must have it rough at home."

Suppressed anger is *misplaced* into the present. It is triggered by a present event—Theodore's note, the car cutting the accountant off, the dog muddying your clothes, pantyhose left in the sink—but its intensity comes from past events.

To know what past event or events might have triggered Bob's response, we would have to know his inner history. But let me suggest that he has—we all have—three different kinds of suppressed anger.

Adult Suppressed Anger

Adult suppressed anger is caused by events that have happened to us since we have been more or less able to defend ourselves against other people.

If Theodore and Bob were feuding over the report, if they had a history of animosity toward each other, if Theodore delighted in putting Bob down, Bob's response to his memo might have been appropriate.

The accountant's detestation of her work could explain—though it probably wouldn't justify—her behavior on the highway.

Adult suppressed anger is a layer deeper than present anger because it has built up over time. It is consequently harder to release. Bob has expressed his anger toward Theodore in this instance, but the force of his response suggests that he is going to feel anger as long as he has to interact with him. If he can't find a way to get that anger out of himself, he would do well to find another job.

Cultural Suppressed Anger

Cultural suppressed anger is harder to define. It is caused by events that affect us less because of who we are as individuals than because we are part of a certain culture. These events happen to us many times—they are endemic to our culture—and certainly started happening before we became adults and able to defend ourselves.

Some women have a lot of suppressed anger about the second-class status of women in our culture. Many women have seen, felt, and experienced the contempt many men feel toward women. A woman's cultural anger may derive its intensity from countless things in her history: the treatment she saw her father give her mother; the consideration her grandparents gave her brother and withheld from her; the attention the elementary school teachers—themselves women!—gave boys as opposed to girls; her high school's emphasis on boys' athletics, which the girls were to feel good cheerleading for. Barbie dolls. Wage discrimination. Pornography. Advertising. Mother-in-law jokes. The defeat of the Equal Rights Amendment.

Had Theodore sent his note to a woman with cultural suppressed anger, he might have stirred up a layer of grievances, fury, shame, and pain that had accumulated in her over her lifetime—maybe even over the lifetime of her mother before her, since her mother was her main role model.

Cultural anger is the form of suppressed anger we can most easily talk about because, even though it is triggered by particular events committed by particular individuals, its causes are prejudices and stereotypes out in the world that all of us can see if our consciousness is raised.

Consider the suppressed anger that members of minority groups in our culture feel at the hostility and prejudice they've suffered in their lives. Think how many of us belong to such stigmatized groups: Blacks, Hispanics, Asians, Arabs, the handicapped, homosexuals, the old, the indigent, the young, the fat, the short, the very tall, left-handers, the red-haired, blondes, atheists, fundamentalists, Catholics, Mormons, Jews, Muslims.

In my workshops I see women who are and admit to being *furious* at men—men in general, not just the particular men who have hurt them. I see men who are *furious* at women—all women.

Most of the bitterness between the sexes comes from cultural anger. Here are twelve cultural reasons why the sexes are angry with each other:

1. Men are angry at women because women are permitted to feel their emotions more than men. Men are envious that women can cry. Men are angry that their own ability to feel has been drilled out of them.

2. Women are angry at men because men won't tell them what they are feeling. When women ask men what they are feeling, men often say nothing or say they don't know. It's often true the men *don't* know, but that doesn't make the women *less* angry.

3. Women are angry that men insist on taking charge. They are angry that when they—women—assert their power, they are called mannish, tomboys, bitches, dykes, ball-crushers. They are angry that our culture expects them to renounce power in the world.

4. Men are angry that women expect them to take charge, pay the bills, quiet women's tears, "fix" women's lives. Men are angry that women hand their power over to them.

5. Women are angry that men use their rage to control them. (Men rage more easily than women.)

6. Men are angry that women use tears to control them. (Women cry more easily than men.)

7. Men are angry that women do their feeling for them.

8. Women are angry that men let them do their feeling for them.

9. Women are angry that men aren't connected to their bodies enough to realize that lovemaking introduces one body into another and so must be done gently and slowly.

10. Men are angry that women always want them to wait, slow down, be "sensitive."

11. Men are angry that women want to change them. Women are angry that men want to change them. Someone else's wanting to change you will always make you angry, because if someone doesn't accept and love you as you are, you feel what you felt as a child: defective.

12. Women are angry that men make them into their mothers, sisters, aunts, past wives and lovers, first girlfriend. Men

are angry that women make them into their fathers, broth-
ers, uncles, past husbands and lovers, first boyfriend.
Someone else's seeing you as someone other than you are
will always make you angry.

A dozen reasons—and there are dozens more.

In our culture, men as well as women are oppressed by sexual
stereotyping. The culture is changing, thank God, and some members
of each sex are acknowledging, even feeling, the pain of the other.
But we all know we have lots of work to do on this issue.

Now, if a woman employee's reaction to Theodore's note were
charged with her anger over the way she had been treated all her life
because she is female or by the fact that Theodore reminds her of
her first husband, who tyrannized her, we can see that she would
likely feel a suppressed anger deeper than the present anger Ellen
felt when she received Edgar's note.

Ellen got her anger out of her system by making a face and swearing
and breathing deeply and setting up an appointment with Edgar to
hear his views and state her own. But how can a woman get rid of
anger that comes less from a boss's note than from her first husband's
behavior or from the fact that she was born female, in America, at
a certain time and place, to a family of certain cultural attitudes?

Short answer: she can't completely.

Longer answer: she can (I'll tell you how later), *but only temporarily*. That anger will come back. She will have to release it again.
And again. She may never be entirely free of it.

How could she be? That anger comes from her history, which can't
be undone. The America she grew up in will always be the America
she grew up in. The first husband she hated will always be her first
husband.

Infantile Suppressed Anger

Infantile suppressed anger is anger that comes from traumatic events
that happened during our first years.

Though many of these incidents happened before we can consciously remember, the anger and grief they provoked are not forgotten. Those feelings are part of our bodies—our members "remember." (The word *remember* calls attention to the way we know our past emotions: through our bodies.)

Many of the most deeply buried events happened before we knew language, so we have no words to express our feelings about them. We will see later that much of the infantile suppressed anger and grief we release from our bodies is expressed as sounds and sobs rather than as words.

If Bob is like most of us, what he learned in his infancy and early childhood was that he wasn't accepted, wasn't cherished, wasn't loved for who he was. He learned not only that the world wasn't made for him, which we all have to learn or be psychotic—constantly out of touch with reality. He learned that, *as he was,* he was insufficient, defective, no good, or never good enough. He learned that if he behaved as his being told him to, people would reject him, punish him, humiliate, ignore, abandon, or leave him, as Theodore did to go skiing.

As I've said, no infant or child can allow himself to be abandoned, because he knows he can't survive by himself. What does the child do when he finds people don't accept him as he is?

The child changes. He tries different behaviors until he finds some that the world accepts. In the words of psychiatrists D. W. Winnicott and Alice Miller, the child adopts a false self because his parents want him to be that way. He suppresses his real self and *pretends* to be someone else.

I have said that the fundamental cause of anger is that the world isn't made to our desire. This fact brings with it a cruel corollary: Because the world is as it is, most of us are forced into not being our real selves.

"Someone else is living my life!" That's the cry of amazement and disgust at the heart of most anger.

"What demon possessed me that I behaved so well?" That's how Thoreau put it.

The fundamental causes of anger are also the fundamental causes of grief, sadness, mourning, lamentation. We are not gods. The world is imperfect. Much as we love it, the world is not made for our delight, and much of what we love best in it perishes, including ourselves. Separation and loss, then, are at the root of human existence. And our worst loss, in many ways, is the loss of what we truly are.

Like the infant in the night who wails to be fed and isn't, these things make us angry, and then they make us sad.

A lot of sadness is connected to deep anger. This is one of the frightening things about it.

In our scenario, Bob reacts to Theodore's note with outrage, not sadness. But we could imagine him being furious for a while and then breaking down in sobs, or being outraged in public and later grieving in private.

I once worked with a man, Larry, whose wife had just left him. He was so mad, he was ready to tear the building down. I was having him express his anger by twisting a towel—one of the ways of releasing anger I'll describe later—when he collapsed in gut-wrenching sobs. He shrieked and sobbed for forty minutes.

It was the primal scream Arthur Janov talks about. Larry had a hole in him that went right down to the bottom. Most of us have a similar hole in us. At the bottom of the hole is the realization that life is not fair, that we don't wholly belong in the world, that we are separated from our parents, our bliss, each other, and God. Throughout our lives countless things reawaken this feeling of abandonment and loss. And like Larry, we rage and weep.

Beneath the bitterest anger, we feel sadness. Beneath sadness, we feel more anger. At the deepest levels, the two are like heads and tails of a coin—you don't have one without the other.

The force of Bob's anger at Theodore suggests that he may have experienced infantile helplessness and abandonment in ways that profoundly marked him. I don't mean to say that he suffered treatment worse than what most of us suffered, although he *may* have. His father may have been domineering and absent, cold, or sexually abusive. We know now that a lot more sexual abuse goes on than we used to think. Psychologists estimate it happens in more than one family in four.

But it doesn't matter whether Bob's childhood was "objectively bad." Feelings aren't objective. What matters is what Bob felt. And the strength of his anger suggests that he felt, and suppressed, infantile anger of great force. This anger bursts out when Theodore's note seems to reject and abandon both Bob and the thing he created to win Theodore's approval, the report.

ANGERS ARE CUMULATIVE, NOT EXCLUSIVE

The three kinds of suppressed anger we have discussed—adult, cultural, and infantile—are of course not mutually exclusive. Bob's response to Theodore's note may be driven by a combination of angers. Theodore's note may seem "bossy" to him and thus remind him of his older brother, or a college teacher who offered him an A if he would sleep with her, all of which reawakens his bitterness toward his authoritarian mother and father.

Were Bob an actual person, he would have all three kinds of anger in him needing release. Like you and me.

II
Getting
Ready to
Release
Your Anger

We have come far enough into our topic to see that if we are to deal with our anger effectively, we have to do two things:

1. Understand as well as we can what causes our anger.
2. Get the anger out of our bodies.

There are many books, such as the anger books I mentioned on page 28, that talk about the causes of anger. There are very few books that tell how to get anger out of the body. This book is doing *both* things.

For the next several chapters, though, I'm going to talk mainly about getting anger out of the body. I'm going to do this, rather than first talk more about understanding our anger, because I think the body is primary. The body *feels* before the mind understands. When it comes to emotions, the mind is a secondary organ interpreting information brought to it by the body.

Not only does the body feel before the mind understands, it also feels *after*. The mind may understand the reason for anger, but as

I've said, this understanding doesn't get rid of the anger. The anger is *in* the body—and understanding why it's there doesn't make it go away. You can know the reason you're furious and still be vibrating with fury. Thousands of people have been through psychotherapy and understand, more or less, what causes their angry feelings. Yet they still feel angry.

Until you get that emotional charge out of your body, you're going to be subject to your anger. The charge may in fact keep you from thinking clearly and thus understanding what causes your anger or what you should do about it. Certainly you'll have trouble making healthy choices if you haven't gotten the anger out of your body.

The mind is secondary in another way. Its work is always inconclusive. We *think* we know the reason we are angry, but we never know for sure. Did Bob get so angry at Theodore's note because his older brother terrorized him, or because he (a handsome man) has never been valued for his intelligence, or because his father (an alcoholic) would suddenly disappear from the family for weeks at a time? It may be one, or more, or none of these reasons. He can't know definitely.

What Bob *can* know definitely is what he feels. When the anger is out of his body, he knows—Ahhh!—it's gone.

The poet Wallace Stevens put the distinction between thinking and feeling very well. "Intellectually we never arrive," he said. "Emotionally we arrive all the time."

4

Expressing Anger: Why We Should Do It and Why We Don't

The last time I got really angry was a month ago. It had to do with this book.

I was driving to the Chattanooga airport to pick up my friend Bill Stott, who is writing this book with me. We had planned to work for three days in a cabin I'd rented in northeast Alabama. It was a cold gray day, and when I was about ten miles from the airport, it began to rain. Right away, it was *pouring*.

I couldn't see too well and missed the airport turn-off. I was on the Interstate and didn't know whether the next exit would allow me to turn around, so I drove off onto the shoulder and started backing up. I'd almost made it to the exit when my back left tire hit a curb with a piece of metal sticking up and blew out.

Okay. There I was, my tire flat, no one around, in the drenching rain, five minutes from the airport, and it was fifteen minutes till Bill's plane arrived. I hadn't changed a tire in ten years—and never on my beautiful, secondhand Volvo. I couldn't find the jack at first. When I finally did, I couldn't find where to put it to lift the car. I was soaking wet. Cars went slashing past me at seventy miles per hour.

I thought, "What would Bev do?" Bev's my woman friend who has good sense about how to keep life orderly.

I thought, "She'd read the owner's manual."

I got into the car, which was nice and warm, and read the manual, which was right where it should be, in the glove compartment. The manual told me how to change the tire. I got out in the rain, changed the tire, and got to the airport only five minutes late.

Bill hadn't arrived yet. His plane was coming from Atlanta, and it hadn't even taken off. In fact, it hadn't gotten to Atlanta yet. The people at the Delta counter couldn't tell me where the plane was and didn't seem to care. "Check back in an hour," they said. "We may be able to tell you something then."

Okay. So I was steaming in the airport, unable to go home because the cabin was forty-five minutes away and Bill might arrive in an hour. I was wet and without a thing to do. *Indefinitely.*

And nobody gave a shit, even though they were being paid to.

I was furious!

"Your book's about anger," I thought. "How do you handle this?"

I ran out to my car, started the engine to get the heater working, and screamed at the top of my lungs. I didn't scream anything in particular for a minute or two, just made a big wail of outrage and complaint. Then I started swearing as loudly as I could.

After a few minutes I was tired and stopped to catch my breath. I laughed for a moment—it was so damned *appropriate* for what I was trying to write. It was the universe saying, "I'll teach you!"

I yelled some more.

Finally I stopped. Took a big breath.

Ahhh!

I shook my body. Gave a couple of big sighs. Yawned.

Then I began thinking about what I could do.

My tire was too wrecked to be repaired, so I needed a new one. I drove off to buy one. And buy a new shirt, which was the only part of me still wet.

Four hours later Bill's plane came in.

"John, I'm sorry," Bill said. "I hope you haven't been waiting."

"It was fine," I said. I meant it. I felt as comfortable as a pussycat.

WHY I FELT BETTER

I felt better because I had gotten my anger out. Screaming and shouting had released it from my body.

Look at what young children do when they're angry or frustrated. They throw themselves on the floor and scream and pound their fists and kick their heels. At least, that's what they do until we punish them for it.

Their reaction is natural. Their bodies are trying to get their anger out, because the body knows that anger isn't healthy when it's stored.

Everyone knows that if you're angry, yelling will make you feel better. True, the psychologists who write about anger say they disagree, but even they say that expressing your anger will make you feel better "momentarily."

Here's what *Of Course You're Angry* says:

Getting mad and yelling, shouting, telling someone off, hitting, or breaking things may make us feel better momentarily, but more often than not these outbursts make us feel worse—much worse, in the long run.

Now, let me say right off that this is a distortion of what I'm going to recommend. *I am* not, *ever, going to say that you should shout at anybody, tell them off, hit them, scold, vilify, hurt, shame, or demean them*. You should *never* do these things unless someone is threatening your life. Such behavior is contemptible and, because it is, may make you ashamed later, as *Of Course You're Angry* says.

But getting into your car and yelling, as I did, doesn't hurt anybody. It doesn't vilify or demean them, as Bob did when he sent Theodore a fax calling him a jackass.

And getting your anger out appropriately makes you feel better. "Momentarily," the anger books say.

All right—it makes you feel better momentarily. For the moment. But that's wonderful! That's everything.

Life is a series of moments, all present. This is true even when, in a present moment, we think of the past or the future.

What *Of Course You're Angry* has acknowledged is that yelling out your anger is—or as the book says, "may be"—a way of feeling better in the present moment.

What this means is that expressing your anger can make you feel better anytime, since anytime you are feeling angry you can find an appropriate way, which doesn't hurt or demean anyone, to express your anger (literally, push it out) and feel better *at that moment*.

If you express your anger and feel better for a moment, then later feel distressed again, you can express your anger again and feel better again for another moment. If you feel distressed again, you can express it again. And so on. And on.

"Momentarily" means always, means forever in the now.

RELEASING ANGER: WHY IT WORKS

To understand why anger release makes us feel better, we have to understand how the emotions work. To understand how the emotions work, we have to understand what they are.

The emotions are energies of different kinds.

We inherited many of these energies—anger, lust, joy, hunger, rage, fear, affection, combativeness, well-being—from our animal forebears. When an animal feels hunger, it "knows" to eat. When it feels fear, it "knows" to protect itself by fighting or fleeing. When it feels lust, it "knows" to procreate. When it feels affection, it "knows" to bond or nurture or protect. When it feels something, it does something about it. Animals don't block or postpone or suppress the energy working in them. They use it up.

And this, ideally, is what we should do. When we feel something—anger or any other emotion—we should express it. *If,* of course, we can do so in a safe and appropriate way.

My yelling in the car made me feel better because it released the anger in my body. Paratroopers feel better screaming "Geronimo!" when they throw themselves out the plane door because the screaming releases some of their fear and tension. Elephants trumpet when they enter into battle.

Just as emotions are natural, so is their physical release.

When their release is inhibited, trouble starts.

ANGER, FEAR, RESENTMENT, HATRED, DESPAIR...

... and all the so-called "negative" emotions are unhealthy when they get caught in the body. They form blocks or knots of stifled energy.

The body knows what is healthy and what isn't, and it wants to release these feelings. But the well-socialized human mind usually won't let it. The mind commands the body to hold those feelings in. The mind says the feelings don't exist, or shouldn't exist for this or that reasonable reason. The mind tries to pray the feelings away or numb them with addictions.

But the mind can't release the feelings. This is not something you can do with your head. A lot of people in Alcoholics Anonymous and other recovery programs know that their health depends on being in touch with their emotions, but they're still trying to do it from the neck up. They're talking the talk, but they haven't gotten their bodies involved. They say, "Hey, I feel great! I've put it all behind me— turned the page. I'm living one day at a time." But notice how tense their jaws are, and their shoulders, neck, arms, hands. You can hear the tightness in their throats.

Their heads are talking. Their bodies are saying something else— "My feelings are safely tied down."

When the mind prevents the body from releasing its "negative" feelings, the body does what it has to: it suppresses the feelings. It stuffs them into a convenient corner, someplace where the body isn't strong enough to reject them. People store their anger variously in their lower back or stomach or jaw or vocal cords or forehead or neck or shoulders or legs or genitals.

A lot of men in this country can't have a full-out orgasm or be wide-open intimate because their *centers*—their bowels, genitals, butts, and lower backs—are too tight with the anger stored there. If a man's gotten angry two thousand times and not done anything about it except stuff it down into his body, how do you expect him to respond when a woman wants to be intimate with him on a sweet night in May? He's so frozen, there's no way into him.

So: the mind prevents the body from releasing its "negative" feelings, the body stores the feelings because it has to, and then . . . ?

Then the body lets the feelings out any way it can, because it has to try to get rid of what's unhealthy. The mind won't let us express the feelings directly, so the body lets them out indirectly. If the feeling is anger, the body lets it out in passive aggression, in sarcasm and ridicule, in misplaced anger—like Bob's fury at Theodore's note— in total, no-holds-barred rage.

When the anger is not released openly, it comes seeping and bursting out in inappropriate ways, at inappropriate times, and often with the wrong people. Many people get rid of some of their anger, as well as their tension and sadness and lust, while having sex. An enormously popular and socially approved way of letting our anger seep out is by being a sports spectator. At a baseball, basketball, or football game it's perfectly all right to shout, "Kill the bastard! Maim him! Stick it in his ear"—even though the real target of our fury isn't on the field but is our spouse or boss or dead parent.

Seeping and bursting is nature's way of keeping us alive. Most of us have stored a lifetime of anger inside us that we can't recall and most likely would deny. The pressure of that anger is such that if we didn't "let off steam" in the inappropriate ways we do, we'd probably be dead of stroke or cancer at twenty-two.

THERE'S A BETTER WAY

A better way of releasing anger than by having it seep or burst out is by consciously and openly expressing it—or rather, allowing your body to express it. Because—again—your anger is in your body, and your body is designed to deal with it.

While you must release the anger in a physical way, this does not need to be loud or violent. As I'll explain in Chapter 6, what you do may be as peaceful as breathing. If your anger is "present anger" of the sort that Ellen felt after Edgar's note, you can probably express it as she did: by making an ugly face or swearing to yourself or breathing deeply or telling someone else your concern.

If your anger is suppressed anger, however, you will probably need to take more drastic action to get it out. But whatever you do, however intense and energetic it is, it definitely shouldn't be and—if you follow my suggestions—*won't* be in the least dangerous or hurtful to you or other people. I'm going to recommend shouting in cars, pounding pillows, kicking sofa cushions—those sorts of things.

Everything I recommend will be safe.

But I know from experience that even safe emotional-release work is deeply threatening to most people. And I want to talk for the rest of this chapter about the resistance we have to doing it.

WHAT KEEPS US FROM HEALTH

There are many reasons why we are reluctant to do emotional-release work. Here are the three big ones:

1. *Ignorance.* We don't know what emotional-release work is, and we don't know how to do it.

That's why I'm writing this book. Keep reading!

2. *Sophistication.* We think we're too good to scream in our car or pound pillows.

We are not too good. Our wish to be "good" causes many of our problems. It makes us pretend to feel what we think we should feel, and it cuts us off from what we really do feel and who we really are.

People who consider themselves too sophisticated to do emotional-release work are talking from their heads, not their bodies. They are denying that they have bodies. They think that because they are intellectually sophisticated, they are emotionally sophisticated too. But they are not.

In fact, no one is emotionally sophisticated. Emotions aren't sophisticated. Emotionally we are all infants. We are one with the elephants, lizards, and protozoa.

Our emotions just *are,* and we are fools not to deal with them as they are and in ways that are responsible and safe.

3. *Fear.*

This is the *biggest* reason.

We know in our bones that anger equals pain, and we're afraid that if we express our anger, we'll hurt somebody or ourselves.

We are right to be afraid of anger, given our histories. When someone tells us it's okay to express our anger in a safe way, we say "Sure," but we don't believe it. How can there be a safe way?

When people in an anger workshop see a huge bearded man pounding on a cushion with both hands as hard as he can and screaming out his anger, or moaning and sobbing, they feel themselves tense the first couple of times. They feel their bodies freeze as they used to when they were children and the anger in the room was meant to hurt someone. If the workshop's competently done, they are totally safe, but they may have to see several people express anger, maybe in several workshops, before their bodies stop shutting down.

Our bodies shut down because what comes out in an anger workshop or when someone is screaming and sobbing in his car, we experience as a potential loss of control.

Emotional-release work frightens us because . . .

EMOTIONAL RELEASE EQUALS LOSS OF CONTROL

And those of us who grew up in dysfunctional families—which is to say, nearly all of us—have never dared to lose control. Our world has always been too dangerous for us to let ourselves be spontaneous or who we really are.

Emotional-release work frightens us, then, because it goes against everything life has taught us. Emotional-release work says, "Let go. Let loose." Our life has taught us, "Hold in. Hold on. Hold back."

Many of us are so constrained that if we're told to do something as safe as make an ugly face, screwing our features up in a distorted way, we can't do it. We can't let go control of the face that our parents and our society and our own aspirations have made us wear, not even for a few minutes among people we trust. We need too much to be in control and show ourselves as the person we *want* to be: good, happy, upbeat, well-adjusted, trustworthy, loyal, faithful, friendly, the 100 percent Scout.

When I asked Walter, a mid-thirtyish account executive for a major Dallas corporation, to make an ugly face, he refused. He said my request was silly, and he'd be even sillier if he went along with it, and he didn't care to look silly. I pointed out to Walter that he had come to see me because his wives (he'd had two) had left him, complaining that he insisted on managing every aspect of their lives. He still wouldn't make a face.

Emotional-release work encourages us to lose control for a number of healthy reasons. If we can't give up control, we're going to spend our lives managing everything, trying to maintain the illusion that we *can* control other people, our environment, and ourselves.

If we are always "in control," life can't happen to us. We can't let ourselves go. We can't learn to swim because we won't give ourselves over to the water. We can't ride a bike because we fear falling. We'll have trouble getting to sleep because we fear helplessness. We can't let ourselves have an orgasm. We can't dance with the wind. We can't cry. We can't feel. We can't die.

Emotional-release work encourages us to lose control—*but in safe and appropriate circumstances.*

Which means, *under control.*

One time I was doing anger work at an outdoor men's retreat. I asked Roger, a two-hundred-pound construction worker, to pound a stick on the ground as hard as he was angry at his mother. Roger yelled, "I'm totally mad, Ma!" as loudly as he could, and on the word "Ma" or just after, the stick hit the ground with a tremendous thud. Yell, thud. Yell, thud. Yell, thud.

Roger kept this up for several minutes—he had lots of anger in him, and he was strong and in great shape. Those of us looking on were getting a bit hypnotized when he turned to me and said in a whisper, "John, would you move back a step?"

I was standing a little close. He was afraid he might hit me!

Even in the middle of his anger, while he was apparently a raging lunatic, Roger knew just what was going on.

He was out-of-control but in control. Just as I had been when I was screaming in my car.

He and I were *safely* out-of-control.

And that's what emotional-release work makes possible.

Once you learn—not only in your head but in your body—that emotional-release work is safe, you'll be on your way to knowing that appropriately expressed anger, yours or other people's, is nothing to be afraid of.

Once you're comfortable with your own anger, you'll stop shutting down when other people are angry in an appropriate—even a semi-appropriate—way. You'll know that their anger is just a feeling in them, and the sooner they get it out, the better.

A SHORT, SAFE EXERCISE

Please go to a mirror now and make ugly faces for three minutes. Don't evaluate or analyze the faces you make. Just *make* them—and look, feel, wonder, laugh, be afraid, be annoyed. Try to really let go and lose control. As you make the faces, move your jaw around and from side to side: most of us store a lot of tension in our jaw. While you're making the faces and after you finish, you'll probably find you yawn a good deal. That's *very* good: Yawning and laughing are two of the nicest ways to release suppressed emotions.

After three minutes of making faces, stop.

Good. Notice you stopped just when you wanted to. You didn't go on forever. You didn't go over the edge. Your face didn't freeze in a hideous position.

Now consider taking this exercise a step further. Find a good friend or partner to make faces at, each of you taking three minutes while the other watches. Again, make the ugliest, most out-of-control faces you can. Yawn, showing all your teeth, fillings, and tonsils.

Notice how you feel: silly, shy, reluctant, ridiculous, whatever. Notice also that the other person stayed, didn't run out the door screaming or call a SWAT team.

After making faces, alone or with a partner, notice how you feel. Isn't your face more relaxed? Losing control a little has its benefits. Being ''silly'' from time to time is good for you—or anyhow, not nearly as bad as many of us fear.

THE TOO-MUCH-ANGER FEAR

If you're afraid your anger or sadness is too enormous to be released safely, don't worry. Hundreds of people have told me things like, ''John, I can't let my anger out because if I ever did, I might tear the building down.'' Most of these people did the emotional-release exercises I suggested and, far from destroying a building, never so much as made a mark on a wall. (The walls we should worry about, incidentally, are those our anger has built in us that separate us from the people we love.)

I must add that a few of the people who were afraid of their anger didn't do the exercises, despite my invitation. They were too frightened, and I of course respected their feeling. I told them they were absolutely right to honor what their bodies told them was right for them. If they were clients, I said I hoped they'd be open to trying an exercise at a later time. If they were members of a workshop, I said I hoped they'd watch other people release their anger and see that nobody was hurt by it.

The point is, no anger is too big to be released safely, so long as the person releasing it isn't already out of control from emotional disorder, drink, or drugs.

THE SPIRITUAL FEAR

My workshops draw a good many spiritual people and New Agers, and some of them don't feel safe expressing their anger because they're afraid of contaminating the world with their "negative" feelings. A few of them have said to me things like, "You're unleashing negativity into the room." Or, "Pillows have feelings too. If you put your anger into them, the universe's pain is just the same as when you had it in you."

I don't know how to answer such people.

I say I also consider myself a spiritual person, and I'm worried about the pain and anger most of us carry around. I figure if I can help people get it out, the universe will be improved.

They say the best thing is for there not to be any anger.

"How are you going to bring up a child and not get angry?" I say. "How are you going to figure your income tax and not start steaming under the collar?"

They say that's why they came to me. I'm supposed to get them over anger.

"But not without *feeling* it!" I say. "Feeling it is the key to getting over it. You're trying to get rid of your anger without having felt it, and you can't do that. The only way to *get over* something is to *go through* it."

"You say you're a spiritual person," they say. "What you're doing by helping people get their anger out is not spiritual work."

That hurts me, because I think it is. I believe that releasing suppressed "negative" emotions enables people to live fuller, more spiritual lives.

Let me tell you my favorite story of what happened to a client of mine when he did anger-release work.

Tony was an ordained minister. He was in his thirties, small-framed, with intense, pale blue eyes. He had been very reluctant to talk about his father at our sessions, much less express his feelings about him. Finally, after weeks of encouragement, he started acting out how he felt by beating a plastic bat on a couch. He pounded away grimly and silently for a long time, as if he were chopping wood. I asked him to put into words what he was feeling, but he didn't say anything. Then this thin squeak, like a child's sound, came from him. "I hate you, Dad. I hate you, Dad. I hate you, Dad." It got louder and more full-voiced, but the words didn't change. "I hate you, Dad. I hate you, Dad." At the end he was bellowing it out. Then he fell onto the couch, weeping, and said, "Because I loved you so much!"

Now, when was Tony the most spiritual? When he was in denial about his anger toward his father? When he was beating the couch and shouting how much he hated him? Or after he was through beating the couch and was overcome by his love for him?

The answer seems obvious to me: after he had gone through the process, come out of denial, felt his rage, released it, and got to his deep hurt and love. He was much closer then to what I call spirituality, and perhaps forgiveness, than he had been before he did the work.

I use this argument with my spiritual critics. I tell them that for many years I tried to be *prematurely* spiritual, just as I tried to be prematurely *nice* with everybody ("Yes, sir, everything is fine, just fine; what can I do for *you*?"). Now, I say, I just try to be human and not frightened of my feelings. And my spirituality feels to me much stronger and deeper.

I know many of my spiritual critics aren't persuaded.

THE FINAL FEAR

The final fear—and the hardest one to beat—is the fear of separation.

A good many people are afraid of doing emotional-release work because they realize their anger toward someone—a parent, a former spouse, a disobedient child grown up—is the only thing that connects them to that person. If they lose the anger, they lose the person and have to deal with the grief of that loss.

I'm particularly sympathetic to this fear because I had it so strongly myself. As I've told you, the first time I was handed a pillow and told to hit it as hard as I was angry at my father, I held the pillow for a minute and then gave it back. I couldn't hit it.

I knew that if I punched the ghost face on the pillow, it would start leaving me. I'd have to realize that my father had *never* been there for me. I'd have to grieve for my abandonment, my lost childhood, the father I'd never had. I'd have to give up the hope that the father I hated would someday love and accept me.

Before I could release my anger, I had to become strong enough to be alone and be myself. I'm still finding out what this means; I'll always be in the process of finding out. Most of us will be. But before I began the process, I was just another rebellious son whose existence centered on hating his father and defying his wishes. Like Will, a young man who stood up during a men's wilderness gathering and said, "If I didn't have my anger at Dad, I couldn't fight him. And that's all I know how to do: fight him. I don't know how to love him."

I've worked with lots of divorced people whose lives are still focused on their ex-spouses. Nothing is left of the marriage but their anger and the grief underneath it, and these people won't give up their anger because between anger and grief, they prefer anger.

What they fear most is facing their grief, facing their abandonment, facing the unfairness of the world. Their anger is their last defense, and many of them won't give it up.

If you won't give it up, you can't release it.

Until you've overcome your fear of the hole at the bottom of your being, you won't be able to get your anger out. So long as you're waiting for someone to give you that apology you deserve and know you'll never get, so long as you're trying to change anybody other than yourself, you're going to be obsessed with anger.

5
Choosing the Proper Target for Your Anger

As I've said, when I ask people in a workshop, "Who are you *really* angry at?" nine out of ten times they say, "Myself."

Deeply angry people have a strong tendency toward self-blame, and often self-destruction. Some try to get their anger out by smashing their fists or even their heads against a wall. Such self-punishment is thoroughly counterproductive. Hurting yourself in any way directs your anger back into you rather than getting it out of your body.

When you punish yourself or mutter to yourself, "You're a disgrace! You screwed things up again!" you stuff more anger into you. The same thing happens if you cover your mouth with your hands and scream how angry you are—you just get angrier.

There may be some occasions when it is appropriate to be angry at yourself, but I don't know what they are. I'm not saying that you don't get angry at what you *do*. You can't avoid this. If you're putting up a picture and mash your thumb with a hammer, you will almost certainly curse and yell. But you shouldn't get angry *at yourself* and call yourself names ("Clumsy shithead") and see the accident as a judgment on you as a person ("You never do anything right").

Ninety-nine percent of the time you should direct your anger outward and toward something else (*"Disgusting* picture! Always hated it"') or someone else—although not usually in that person's presence.

Let me give you an example. You blow your stack and punish your child hard for a minor infraction of the rules. The next day, you tell your best friend or therapist, "I've made a mistake, and I'm very angry with myself and ashamed of myself for doing it.'' The friend or therapist asks you why you did it. Whether or not you have an explanation, you continue to berate yourself. All this runs counter to the healing process. What you are doing is bringing up anger and thrusting it back into your body.

The question to be asked isn't "Why did you mistreat your child?" because there can't be a good reason for treating a child badly. Rather, the question is "Who taught you to act like that?"

If you ask yourself this question frankly and think about the mistreatment you received as a child, you'll say, "Hm. Well, my dad used to act like that." Or your mom. Or your aunt. Or Reverend Spencer, when he'd come over to your house. Whoever taught you to act that way—whoever "modeled the behavior" for you, as psychologists say—is the appropriate target for your anger.

Most of the time when you do something that makes you angry—get drunk, kick your dog, hang out with riffraff, postpone writing a paper until it's too late to do a good job, fail to ask for a raise or the last piece of cake—you're following a pattern set up for you in your youth. You have every right to be angry with whoever modeled the pattern for you or forced you to embrace it. When you do anger-release work, it is completely appropriate to yell that person's name and to curse him or her.

Once you recognize the source of the pattern you're repeating, you take the first step toward breaking it. You learn that it is not intrinsic to you: It's a bad habit you picked up, not a bad or defective you. Now you know the proper object for your screams, shouts, curses, and vilifications during anger-release: Dad, Mom, Aunt Elizabeth, or Reverend Spencer.

Other writers on anger would argue that when you say, "I'm pissed off at you, Dad, for teaching me that behavior," you're not taking responsibility for your own actions. But they're wrong. You didn't come into the world intending to be a tyrant to your child—somebody had to make you believe such behavior was right. You are now taking responsibility for working to see that the behavior isn't perpetuated. You have said, "I'm going to find out why I did such a thing. I'm going to feel my feelings about it and who-ever taught me to do it. And then I'm going to get the necessary skills, education, information, retraining, whatever, so I don't do it again."

If, instead of doing this, you blame yourself, you simply push your angry and self-loathing energies back inside, and then have to use *more* energy to hold them in place. Further, you reinforce the dys-functional behavior you dislike and make it more difficult to change by accepting that it is fundamentally *your* behavior.

Your self-blame—"I'm disgusted with myself and furious and sick at heart"—is closer to self-pity than it is to taking responsibility for what you've done, felt, learned, and now mean to change. If you excoriate yourself in the presence of your child, hoping thereby to apologize to him or her, you risk perpetuating the problem, because your child is likely to learn to direct anger at himself or herself, as Daddy or Mommy did.

Even though you target your anger at the person who taught you a dysfunctional pattern of behavior, you realize that in reality that person is probably no more to blame for it than you are. He or she was also a victim and learned the dysfunctional pattern of behavior from someone else, who was also a victim who learned the behavior from someone else. And so it goes, back and back.

This is why you should be proud of taking the initiative to break the pattern now. If your pattern is overreacting to your child's mis-behavior, getting your anger out of you appropriately, away from your child, using exercises like those I'll give you in Chapter 6, is a spiritual act that breaks the chain of your parents' and their parents' and our culture's wrongheaded treatment of children.

As a young mother I know likes to say, "There are some mistakes that are going to stop with *this* generation."

THE REAL TARGET ISN'T A WHO BUT A *WHAT*

In most cases, your real anger is directed at a pattern of behavior, not at an individual person. This should give you even more freedom to release your anger, if you still are fearful about doing it.

Though the object of your anger has a person's name, face, and history, you aren't attacking the person because:

- The person isn't present.
- The person isn't to blame.
- Something the person did—and not the person himself or herself—is the object of your attack; and
- The person is no longer the person who did the thing you're attacking.

Your anger is with your parent in 1962, not with your parent in 1993. It's important not to confuse your parent today with the ghost parent of your childhood. For instance, you should not call up your sixty-five-year-old father living in South Florida and say, "I just mistreated my child the way you mistreated me, you son of a bitch. I hate your guts."

It is *fine* to hate your parents or anyone else who has done you wrong; whatever feelings you have are fine. But the pattern of behavior you hate was modeled or forced on you by your ghost parent. Your quarrel is with him or her, and it is him or her you must confront: your parent as he or she was when the wrong was committed. Your parent today isn't responsible for mistakes short of felonies that were made thirty years ago. He or she probably wouldn't remember or understand what you're shouting about. Doing anger-release work will help you separate your ghost parents from your parents today and may substantially improve your relation to your parents today.

While you no doubt have quarrels with your parents as they are today, the anger these quarrels produce in you is *present* anger and can be dealt with directly and appropriately, so long as you take care not to mix your present anger with your buried rage.

What if your parents are dead? What if you have *only* ghost parents and none today? Because your deepest anger comes from the past, you stand as good a chance of making your peace with your parents dead as alive. Indeed, it may be easier to make peace if they're dead, since you won't be sidetracked by their current behavior. As the poet Robert Bly says, you can have a better conversation with a dead parent than a live one.

Because those ghost parents are *in you*. That's the only place they are. And you can do anything you want to with them. You can have them crying and apologizing (finally!), saying they never meant to hurt you as they did. They can beg your forgiveness and hug and kiss you and promise to do better. You can tell them it's too late and watch impassively as they crawl out of the room on their hands and knees.

You hold these negative parents for whom you were never good enough within you. You can get rid of these bad ghosts. Your *good* ghost parents—the ones who cared for you and taught you healthy things, like how to care for yourself—you will always have with you.

III
Getting Your Anger Out

I'm going to do now just what I'd do at this point in an anger workshop: an exercise to get us into some deep feelings.

An exercise like this is tough to do in a book. It's easy in a workshop to address our feelings, but writing like this mainly addresses our minds. Of course, intellectual escapists like us are happy to *think* about things so long as we can avoid experiencing them. We feel infinitely safer in our heads than in our bodies.

You know the story: On the way to heaven are two paths. The sign on one path says "Paradise." The sign on the other path says "Lecture About Paradise." And everybody takes the second path! Even in heaven we'd want to be in control. We just wouldn't be sure God had our best interests at heart.

So take a slow, deep breath. . . . Exhale.

Again.

Three more times.

Read the rest of this sentence, and then close your eyes for a minute or so and keep breathing deeply.

THE POINT OF WHAT WE'LL DO NOW...

... is to help ease us past some mental blocks and into our feelings.

Get something to write with, a pen or pencil, and some paper. Give yourself at least half an hour to work on this exercise.

Imagine you are in a group of people in a quiet room. Someone's talking in a soothing voice:*

"First of all, I want you to know you are safe. Nothing bad, nothing at all threatening is going to happen to you. If you feel the least unsure about what we're doing, stop doing it. Just sit there and keep breathing.

"All right. Now take a full, deep breath. . . . Exhale. Take another deep breath. Let it out. . . . As you breathe out, relax every part of your body. . . . Completely. Close your eyes. Let your attention sink down into your body as your breath sinks down. . . . Focus on your chest now. Breathe. Feel your chest and neck relax as you breathe out. . . . Now focus on your stomach. Breathe in and out. Let your attention fall into your legs and feet. Feel your body and stay in it. . . .

"Picture your mother when you were a child. See her. Remember how she dressed and how she sounded. . . . Hear her. . . . Smell her. . . . Touch her. . . .

"As you remember her and keep breathing, I'll give you three words to say three times. Say them quietly to yourself. Keep the words *inside* you for the moment.

"The first word is 'Mother.' . . . While taking full, deep breaths, say 'Mother' to yourself three times.

" 'Mother.' . . . Let your attention wander through your entire body. . . . You've got all the time in the world. 'Mother.' . . . Does the word let you feel the knots in your body where you store your anger or sadness? What memories does the word bring up?

" 'Mother.' . . .

"Now say 'Mom' three times as you breathe and pay attention to

---

*You may want to read these words into a tape recorder and then play them back while you do the exercise.

your body the same way. . . . 'Mom.' Feel your body and stay in it. . . . 'Mom.' . . . Observe the memories that come up. . . . 'Mom.' . . .

"Now say 'Mommy' . . . and keep breathing. 'Mommy.' . . . 'Mommy.' . . .

"Now add the word 'my' before these three words. 'My mother.' . . . 'My mom.' . . . 'My mommy.' Move gently through your body, seeing what feelings and memories are there.

"Now, slowly, staying in touch with what you've felt in your body, take up your pen or pencil and write what you felt. Write whatever scenes or memories come up. Maybe there's one that's most important to you now. Write it. Use the first words that come to mind. . . . Take all the time you want. . . .

"Okay. Pause for a moment. Stretch and shake your body up. Yawn, if you can—yawning is as healthy as laughing or crying. *Big* yawns. Keep breathing.

"Now write a letter to Mommy or Mom or Mother and tell her what you learned from revisiting your feelings about her. Tell her what comes first and strongest to you. Don't worry if you're criticizing her; say just what you feel. . . .

"How was that?

"Scary? Is that what you said? But not *scary* scary, right? *Good* scary. Powerful scary. True scary. Emotional."

IT GETS EMOTIONAL IN A WORKSHOP

Some people cry during this exercise as they pay attention to their bodies and take time to feel what their mother means to them. A few people start growling, but most people feel that their anger is so dangerous, they keep the growls in.

"Mother" and "Father" and their offshoot words are among the most powerful words we humans have. But they lose much of their force when they are written on paper rather than felt as part of a person's body.

Anger work, emotional-release work, can't be done in your head. I'm talking about it here, from my head to your head, because that's what I have to do in a book. But even if you think my ideas make some sense, you won't *know* whether they do until you try them out in your body.

Did the little exercise we did put you in your body? Did you feel some knots of suppressed emotion in you about your mother and reexperience what caused those emotions?

As I say, a workshop makes it easier for people to get a little out of their heads and into their bodies. A workshop is a way of getting in touch with your suppressed feeling safely and in public, as are support groups and, most of all, intimate friendships.

But at every workshop I do, there is one person, almost always a man, who announces that he can't get to his feelings. "Damn, I wish I could get angry," he says. "Everybody else is doing it, and I can't. I'm a failure at this too!"

I tell the man there isn't any "failure" in emotional-release work because it is wholly individual. I say he is taking care of himself in just the right way for him at that time.

I ask whether he feels safe with what is going on in the room—whether he feels he or other people are being hurt by the emotions expressed.

"No, I see it's safe," the man says. "I just want to do it."

I then ask if he'd try an exercise. I have him pound a pillow or twist a towel while saying, "I want to do it!" or, "I want to get angry!" or whatever he's said to me. In my experience, *the expression of the emotion*, the angry pounding or twisting and the angry tone of voice, *always brings the emotion up*. And the man who said he couldn't reach his anger winds up shouting with it.

(The first person to point out that the expression of an emotion makes us feel the emotion was William James. I quoted him earlier as saying that the *contrary* is also true: if you "refuse to express a passion," the passion "dies." This is *not* true.)

When the man who couldn't get to his anger finishes the exercise, always—again, in my experience—he's able to report what he thinks caused the emotion he expressed. It might be a whipping he received, or the time he, a boy of six, was sent alone on a twenty-hour bus ride and feared there'd be nobody to meet him at the other end. It might be his hatred of his parents' strict morality, which kept him from dating the girls he wanted to date.

The process of expressing an emotion brings up memories of the events that caused it. *Getting to our feelings and expressing them generally helps us discover their probable causes.*

IF YOU CAN'T GET TO YOUR FEELINGS

The men and women in the workshops who say they can't get to their feelings are usually 95 percent ready to start feeling. The fact that they speak up in public means they want to take the plunge. They are challenging me to encourage them, which I do, gently. And that's all that's needed.

I'm well aware, however, that other people in the workshop, perhaps many of them, women as well as men, are not able to get to their feelings but don't speak up about it.

If the "Mother" exercise didn't stimulate feelings in you, you may be afraid you can't get to your suppressed feelings.

But don't worry.

You can. You *do.*

Life puts each of us in touch with our suppressed feelings more often than we'd like. Life exhumes whatever we have buried inside us. When Bob got Theodore's note, he was given the opportunity to deal with anger left over from his past. So was the accountant when the car cut her off. So was I when Bill Stott's plane was late.

Life makes us confront feelings we want to deny. The more we struggle to "escape" the feelings, the more certainly we will have to face them. Psychologist Harville Hendrix argues—correctly, I think—that we are drawn to relationships with people who will wound us in the same way our parents did, so that we will have the chance to feel the hurt again and try to heal it. If we haven't dealt with our parents' abandoning us, say, we will keep setting ourselves up to be abandoned by other people. We will fall in love with people like our parents, hoping to hold them this time. Which we will usually fail to do, precisely *because* they are like our parents.

When we run from certain feelings, we set ourselves up to be knocked over by them again.

So if you can't consciously put yourself in touch with your feelings, have no fear: They will get in touch with you. But they will do so in the messy way life works. The feelings will come too suddenly, and in ways too confusing and strong to be dealt with. You'll be in touch with your feelings, but you won't be safe. And you'll be likely to make the same mistakes again.

That's why I recommend emotional-release work.

Emotional-release work is a safe way of reexperiencing the emotions we hate and fear, of reviving—at a safe distance—pain from the past that was so great when it first happened that we shut down. Emotional-release work removes those old poisons, those blockages, from our body and psyche to permit the smooth flow of energy so we can really be alive in the present.

I feel pretty sure that using the exercises I give in the next chapter you will be able to get in touch with some of your suppressed feelings and release them in the privacy of your own room. While not all the exercises will work for you, I'm quite confident that at least one or two will. If *none* does, if you try them and find you aren't able to get in touch with your feelings, then I'd recommend you consider joining a support group or workshop dealing with emotions. You may need the stimulus of other people's feelings to move you into your own. You were hurt and you shut down among other people. You may need to see that people can have and express their emotions openly and safely with one another before you'll be comfortable enough with your emotions to feel them in private. For some people, it's easier being intimate in public than with themselves.

Alternatively, you may need a therapist to encourage you. I'll come back to the question of therapists in Chapter 7.

6
Anger-Release
Exercises

This chapter gives you exercises and techniques that I use myself in my workshops on anger. These exercises are intended to put you in touch with your feelings and help you discharge them.

Not all the exercises will work for you, but that doesn't matter. You are looking for the ones that do, because you will be able to use them again and again. Our emotions being subjective and changeable, an exercise that works for you, done at different times, will bring up different feelings and accompanying memories.

BREATHING

Breathing is the royal road to being in your body, and to healing.

Whenever I'm feeling nervous, threatened, oppressed, mournful, empty, "blue," "low," or "down in the mouth," I take a couple of deep, full-bodied breaths, in and out, and usually that's enough to bring my spirits back to equilibrium.

Breathing increases the energy in your body and allows that energy to move freely and be evenly distributed, so your brain or stomach isn't outrunning the rest of you.

Furthermore, if you're feeling something and you consciously keep breathing, you will be able to stay with that feeling until you've experienced it fully and it passes from you. If you stop or diminish your breathing, you will diminish the emotional experience.

You've probably noticed that people who are afraid hold their breath—they don't want to feel the emotion that's overcome them. As children, we would stop breathing and go numb to avoid the pain of what was happening to us. When we stopped breathing, however, we turned ourselves into passive victims. The abuse entered our body without us putting up a fight, and because we didn't fight it, it dug further into us.

If someone is attacking you and you keep breathing deeply, you won't take in much of their anger because your body's being filled with *your* energy and isn't open to the other energy in the room. Even if the other person's anger is unsafe, inappropriate, and out to hurt you, you'll be able to handle most of it, so long as it's not violent. If their anger is appropriate, reasonable, and nonblaming, you'll be able to handle all of it.

The same is true with your own anger. If you're expressing it and you stop or reduce your breathing, some of the anger coming out of you will go back in and you'll get scared.

Imagine that a man is with a woman he loves and he is working toward feeling his feelings when the woman suddenly sucks in air and holds her breath. The man thinks, "What's wrong? What have I done?" He's afraid because the woman's telling him with her body, "Don't have these feelings. I can't handle them. I can't be with you." If the man keeps breathing, he'll be okay, even if he can't get his feelings out in her presence. But if he doesn't breathe, he'll be overcome with fear. He'll join her in her numbness.

When you're scared, remember—take a deep breath. Like a seven-year-old who is jumping off the diving board for the first time.

I've taught the technique of conscious, deep breathing to people who are in loving but argumentative relationships. These people tell me now that their partner can be chewing them out, and so long as they concentrate on breathing, they feel fine. By breathing fully, they tell their partner, "I'm okay. I can deal with this. I can be with you, baby, come rain or come shine."

Deep breathing is being there. And being yourself there. And controlling how close you want other people to come to you.

Let me tell you now how to breathe deeply. It's simple, but it needs to be done right.

Breathe in slowly, through your nose, until your stomach pushes out nearly as far as it will go. We Americans are very stomach conscious—we want to hold ours in. Well, you can't breathe deeply and hold in your stomach.

How often should you breathe deeply? Whenever you think of it— but especially when you feel threatened or oppressed in some way. You can breathe deeply as much as you want to *so long as you breathe slowly*. If you breathe deeply *fast,* you'll hyperventilate and get light-headed from too much oxygen. That's why you breathe in through your nose: to cut down on the speed and thus the amount of air you inhale.

I breathe deeply at different times throughout the day but by no means all the time. Deep breathing has become more automatic the more I've done it, but I probably still do it less than two hours a day all told. I consciously do some deep breathing every morning before I get out of bed, and it gives me energy and confidence.

When I realize I've been under stress, I sit down somewhere and do yoga breathing. This is the same kind of full-bodied breathing, except that I close my eyes and add counting to it. I breathe in slowly, through my nose, counting to four. I hold my breath, counting to two. I exhale slowly, through my nose, counting to four.

When I breathe this way for a couple of minutes, I become very calm. I enter a meditative state in which I sometimes see a past event with fresh eyes and find connections between it and emotions buried in me.

Breathing is crucial to emotional-release work. By itself, breathing is often sufficient to release mild present angers. If you're hitting every traffic light, or if the man ahead of you in the nine-item express lane at the grocery has thirteen items (you counted!), try breathing in and out deeply a few times and see if your anger doesn't seep away.

In summary, breathing (1) defends us against other people's feelings, while communicating to them that they are free to feel their feelings; (2) increases our energy, to get us over the blues and the blahs; and (3) enables us to stay in our bodies and feel what we're feeling, however mild or strong these feelings are.

A Safe, Simple Exercise

To show you the healing power of breathing, let me suggest you find a comfortable place to sit where the light's not too bright. Loosen any tight clothing you have on, and begin breathing full, deep, slow, calm breaths. In and out. Close your eyes. As you breathe, let any thoughts, pictures, memories come up that want to. Let your mind roam. Don't only *see* what your mind brings you—hear the sounds, smell the smells. Keep breathing.

After twenty breaths or so, you may feel a little light-headed. This is okay and normal—nothing to worry about. Continue breathing slowly and calmly, but a little less deeply.

Now turn your mind to a time in your childhood when you were a little scared or anxious. Don't think of a *terrible* incident, just one where you felt alone and unsure what to do. I have a picture of me at thirteen with my hair slicked in a pompadour, my shoulders hunched, my hands stuck in my jeans, and the most awful trying-to-be-relaxed smile on my face. I remember how miserable I felt when the picture was taken, how much I wanted to come out looking the way I wanted to look.

Think of yourself in a similar position. Recall the details of the scene: where you were, who was there, what the weather was like, how the air felt, what sounds you heard. Keep breathing.

Now tell yourself *as you were then* to relax and breathe with you. Slowly, calmly, deeply. Encourage your child-self until that child is breathing as easily and fully as you are now. See the child-you become less scared and rigid and *victimized*. A part of you is that child, and simply by thinking and breathing, you can make that child healthier in your mind.

TALKING

Thanks to Freud, we are accustomed to the idea that we can deal with our psychological problems by talking them out.

This is true and not true.

Like breathing, talking is a fine way to express and release present anger. Ellen gets over her anger at Edgar's note in part by talking to his secretary and making an appointment to talk with Edgar about the report as soon as he returns. Her first words to him might be, "I must say I was upset at your note saying the report wasn't what you wanted, and I'm glad we're going to hash things out now."

In later chapters I will talk about appropriate ways of expressing your anger to whoever caused it. The crucial thing to make clear now is that many angers are too strong to be talked out right away with the person who caused them or apparently caused them. Talking can express present anger, but it usually can't handle deeply suppressed anger.

On the other hand, talking *about* your anger—present or suppressed—is enormously helpful, provided you do it with a safe person: that is, someone who won't be hurt by whatever you say or try to hurt you for having said it.

Let's say Sue is angry at Steve because he was late picking her up for the second time that week. She might say to him, "I'm feeling really steamed, but I'm not sure how much it's about your being late or if it's connected to other stuff. I've got to sort out my feelings before I say anything more."

Because her anger is strong, Sue doesn't talk to Steve about it. Instead, she talks about it with someone else, perhaps her best friend, her therapist, maybe her twelve-step group, or perhaps herself—in her journal. Talking to someone else clarifies Sue's feelings because an outside person who's uninvolved can listen and be somewhat objective, or at least supportive. Sue may not want advice. She may just want to express her anger and be accepted as angry. Her excited talk, sympathetically listened to, may be enough to heal her. If she wants advice and asks for it and the uninvolved person offers it, then the process has become reality checking, which I'll discuss later.

Once the intensity of Sue's anger is gone, she can return to Steve and say, "Honey, I was angry. I think I understand the reason now. In any case, I feel fine." If there's a reason to, she can even use that dangerous word *because*. "Honey, I was angry because you were late again. If you're going to be late, please call and tell me. I always have work I can do. But I see that the reason I was so pissed wasn't really about you. It was about me, remembering being a latchkey child twenty years before the term was invented and waiting and waiting for my mom to come home when she said she would."

Talking, then, like breathing, can release a present anger. Talking with a safe, sympathetic person can release anger that is suppressed but not deeply buried.

And, of course, talking with a safe person is helpful in *understanding* angers of all kinds and depths. As I've said before, though, understanding anger doesn't release it from our bodies. To do this, we may need more physical expression.

WRITING

Writing is like talking. It can release present and slightly buried anger, and it can lead to understanding anger of all levels, even the very deepest. Its advantage over talk is that—no surprise here—you can do it alone.

Psychologists have recently done experiments that suggest that people who write about their most troubling experiences and innermost feelings may be healthier, both physically and mentally, than those who don't. James Pennebaker at Southern Methodist University conducted studies in which participants wrote for twenty minutes over four consecutive days. One group of participants wrote about their traumatic experiences, often things they had never discussed before. The topics they wrote on included sexual abuse, suicide attempts, and paralyzing guilt and shame over things they'd done. The other group of participants wrote on superficial topics, like a description of the room they were in.

Pennebaker found that those who wrote about their traumatic experiences for several months thereafter visited doctors and psychologists much less often than they had before and significantly less often than the people who wrote on trivial topics.

In another study, Janice Kiecolt-Glaser and Ronald Glaser at Ohio State University found that people writing about traumatic experiences had many more T-cells in their blood than people writing on unemotional topics. T-cells help fight bacterial and viral infection.

Another psychologist, Edward J. Murray of the University of Miami, has done a study that suggests that "just writing about emotional experiences . . . seems to produce as much therapeutic benefit as sessions with a psychotherapist."

These researchers believe that autobiographical writing that tells painful truths is healthful for two reasons. Pennebaker:

> It reduces the physical and mental stress involved in inhibiting thoughts. But more importantly, writing is a powerful tool to organize overwhelming events and make them manageable. The mind torments itself by thinking about unresolved issues. By translating the experience into language, people begin to organize and structure the surge of overwhelming thoughts. Once organized, they are easier to resolve.

I am prepared to believe these claims because after I finished writing my painful autobiography, *The Flying Boy: Healing the Wounded Man*, the insomnia, headaches, and stomach problems that had plagued me all my adult life disappeared. My claim, though, is simply that heartfelt confessional writing will put you in touch with your suppressed feelings and suggest what may have caused them.

Let me offer six writing exercises you may want to try.

Before you do any of these exercises, be sure to sit quietly for a couple of minutes, breathing deeply and letting your mind wander through your body. As you write, concentrate on what you're writing about, and try to feel it, remembering that the way to get in touch with your feelings is to *keep breathing*.

1. List of Dysfunctions

Make a numbered list of all the dysfunctional things you do. Make the list as long as you can.

Then go back and concentrate on each item in the list, one by one. Feel what that item makes you feel. Then write down beside it an *M* or an *F*, depending on whether your mother or your father did the same thing. If both your mother and father did it, write down both *M* and *F*.

2. Sentence Completion

A variation on the above. Complete the sentences:

When Dad got angry, he . . .
When Mom got angry, she . . .
When I got angry as a child, I . . .

Which parent are you most like? You may be surprised how much of what you do was modeled for you by your parents. As the old saying has it, "Children don't take after strangers."

A couple of chapters ago, I said I was proud I never hit a woman because I broke my father's behavior pattern in that way. I didn't say then, and I should have, that I used to do like my daddy and hit and kick domestic animals. I'm pleased to say that emotional-release work has cured me of that destructive behavior.

3. Description of Your Abandonment

Write about a time you were abandoned. Or write about the time you were saddest.

For this exercise, if you're right-handed, write with your left hand. If you're left-handed, write with your right hand. Writing with the opposite hand will get you out of the logical, dominant side of your brain and into the dream side, where your emotions are. If you're right-handed and write with your right hand, you're likely to write words that justify and rationalize away your anger and pain. Your left hand is more likely to speak from the gut. Our opposite hand usually speaks for the child in us.

Don't worry if your writing is sloppy. You're the only one who's going to see it. Breathe and relax as you're writing. Don't try to rush through this exercise, because it will take time for your opposite hand to do this unaccustomed task. Let your hand talk to you.

4. List of People You're Angry At

List everybody you're angry at, and put down the reasons. Go as far back in your memory as you can. No reason is unreasonable—if you feel angry, you're angry. No incident is too small—if you recall it, it's memorable. Even *tiny* things can have huge consequences.

In a men's group I was running, one man couldn't get to his deep anger. He'd expressed anger but all from his head. I noticed on his list, way down, he'd written, "Second grade, Alison left," with a question mark.

I said, "Who's Alison? Why the question mark?"

He told me that in second grade he'd had a sweetheart, Alison. They were neighbors and played together all the time. One day he came to school, and she wasn't there. He went to her house, and her family was gone. They had moved.

He had been carrying that anger and hurt for thirty years, thinking that he "shouldn't be angry" . . . "It wasn't really important" . . . "That's the way life is" . . . "Adults don't care about such things."

And in those thirty years he hadn't married. He hadn't been able to open up with a woman. Alison's unexplained departure, an event that had seemed totally unimportant, had been influencing him all that time. When he got close to a woman, he'd pull back because he was afraid that someday she just wouldn't be there.

The other members of the group and I encouraged him to feel Alison's loss, and he started weeping. He raged at his parents and the school and at Alison's parents and Alison. He cried, "I just wanted to know where she *was*! I wanted to say good-bye, at least." It was touching. I and a couple of the other men cried with him, remembering our hurts.

You need to know what really matters to you. When you've made a list, add things to it as they come to mind. Whatever comes to mind is operative in your emotional life.

Again, what matters to you doesn't have to be something you *respect*, something "mature" and "reasonable." What matters to you probably won't be mature and reasonable, because our emotions aren't either of those things. It doesn't matter whether other people care about what you care about, because *you* care about it. It doesn't matter whether you *want* to care about it, because *you do*.

Maybe you had a teddy bear that got lost when you moved. Or a gym teacher who ridiculed you. A preacher who told you you were a sinner at twelve. A music teacher who told you not to sing with the rest of the class because you couldn't stay on key. A pet that was put down that you still miss.

Whatever you're angry about, respect that feeling enough to stay with it, let it work on you. You may be so moved that you need to express your emotion by screaming or beating a pillow or twisting a towel or doing another of the physical exercises I'll talk about in a moment.

5. Letter Writing

With your opposite hand, write a letter to someone you're really angry at: your mom or dad or both of them; your spouse, your lover, your ex-spouse; your first love, your child, your boss. It doesn't matter whether the person is living or dead because you're writing the letter for yourself, not them, and you're never going to send it.

In the letter, use whatever language comes out of you first. Be as vile, contemptuous, and blaming as you feel like. Tell the person you're writing *why* you're so angry. Go into all the details. All of them—don't try to protect their feelings. Keep breathing!

If you stay in your feelings long enough to write the letter, your body will probably remember other experiences that contribute to the depth of your emotion. These experiences will not necessarily involve the person you're writing your letter to, but include them in the letter anyhow. They may give you another person to be angry at, thus uncovering another layer of your anger.

When you've finished that letter, if you're still furious, write another. To the same person or whomever you then feel most angry at. About a year ago I wanted to write my father, with whom I hadn't been in touch for three years. I wrote maybe twenty letters before I could write one that wasn't vicious in its anger. The earlier letters were written to hurt my father—and maybe still with the childhood wish to change him. But those letters did what they were supposed to do: They changed *me* by giving me access to my anger and the chance to experience and express it.

Keep writing letters as long as you've got the anger to do so. Keep writing and breathing until you feel your body go, "Ahhh! That's it. Enough. I feel better."

Which doesn't mean, of course, that your anger is gone for good—just that it's gone for now. When feelings of anger and oppression come up again—later that day, the next week, in a month—you may want to write more letters.

But for now you have released that anger from your system.

6. Journal Keeping

Begin to keep a journal.
And tell the truth in it!

Most journals are written by people presenting themselves as they want to be seen. As though somebody else were going to read what they wrote. Journal writers realize that what they write isn't going to be read right away—maybe not until they're dead. But still! What are people going to think *then*? The writers want to have their best face on.

It is *very* hard to get over our need to appear good in other people's eyes. Psychologists estimate that more than one-third of people in psychotherapy never reveal things about themselves that trouble them because they don't want to alienate their therapists. It is surprising that private journals share the same censorship, but they do. If journaling is to be of real use to us in understanding our emotions, we have to break through the masks of propriety and "good taste" to the feelings that seethe beneath.

PHYSICALLY EXPRESSING ANGER

The breathing, talking, and writing exercises I've just explained will bring up your feelings, and sometimes the feelings will be too intense, too *big* to be discharged by these exercises. You will need to do something physical to get rid of the feeling—anger, for example.

How will you know *how* angry you are? By paying attention to your body. If you're really angry, you'll find your voice is squawking or shouting, your stomach is in knots, your arms are thrashing the air.

How can you tell *where* your anger is located? By noticing what part of you remains knotted when you're breathing deeply with the rest of your body relaxed. By observing where you get recurrent pains—in your head, neck, back, bowels. By seeing the way you talk about your anger ("The whole thing makes me sick to my stomach," or "I've had it up to here with him") or about violent things you'd like to do. A woman in an anger group announced that she wanted to "kick my boss's butt all the way to Albuquerque." That suggested to me that a lot of her anger was in her legs, so I had her lie down on a couch and kick it as hard as she could.

The part of your body where you have stored your anger is the part that has to express it. If your anger is located in your jaw or throat or stomach, for example, screaming or coughing or yawning will get it out better than pounding a pillow. If your anger is in your arms or shoulders, pounding a pillow will release it better than screaming.

(By the way, when you feel a knot of anger or sadness or any emotion in a part of your body, you can speak directly to it in your mind and invite it to speak to you. Say something like, "Tell me what you feel. Don't be afraid. Say whatever you want to. I'm not afraid. Speak up." In my experience, what the knot wants to tell you will then usually cross your mind.)

As you try the physical exercises I suggest, you're going to feel what people in my anger workshops sometimes feel, and maybe you'll want to say what they say to me: "This is silly! I'm just *acting*. I don't really believe what I'm doing, so it can't do me any good."

My answer to you is the same as my answer to them: Yes, you are acting to some degree. That's unavoidable and *fine*. The exercise will almost certainly still work. In a five-minute exercise where you're releasing anger, if you suddenly get sincere and, without meaning to, semi-lose control and really *do* what you're doing without thinking about it, *even for ten seconds*—as nearly everybody does, because the mind gets tired fighting to stay in control—that is worth the whole effort. That is incredibly powerful and healing.

Okay. When your anger is too big to be expressed from the body by breathing, talking, or writing . . .

1. Scream in the Car

Get in your car, roll up the windows, and scream as loudly as you can.

How long should you scream? As long as you have the energy to. I find that after an initial burst of screams, I always laugh for a couple of seconds, though I'm not sure why. Maybe because I've been suppressing joy under my anger. Maybe because my body's happy that I'm letting it do something so healthy. Maybe because I'm still amazed that screaming makes me feel better so fast. After the laughs, I go back to screaming. Until I don't feel the need pressing on me to scream anymore at that time because that wave of anger is used up.

A former client of mine who's restless in his marriage tells me he screams every morning while driving to work. He screams at the start of the trip till the pressure of his anger leaves him. Then he thinks about other things. Then, three to five minutes after the first series of screams, when thoughts about his marriage return, he screams again. He says he's never been so happy. (I say, "That's great. Now when are you going to work on the marriage?")

This exercise is particularly good for me because I store anger in my throat and my gut.

If you don't have a car handy, take a pillow and scream into it. You can do this in an apartment and the neighbors won't hear.

When you're screaming in the car or into a pillow, it is completely appropriate for you to say *anything* you need to to get your anger out. Use blaming, hurtful, or accusatory words, obscenities, curses—whatever. Name names. Verbally expressing violent feelings gets them out of you for the moment and, no less important, reminds you that they are *in* you and that you must recognize the dark side of your nature.

You of course understand that you must not say any of these things near somebody who might be hurt by them.

2. Twist a Towel

Take a bath towel in both hands, and twist it as tightly as you can. As you twist your anger into the towel, let out any sighs, moans, or grunts that come up. Or repeat, "I'm angry!"

Imagine the tension in your body being discharged through your arms and hands into the towel. When you finish, the towel will have knots in it that used to be in you and now are not.

This is a good exercise if you store anger in your shoulders, neck, hands, and arms.

If you store anger in your jaw, bite the towel as you twist, and make growling sounds.

Towel twisting makes a nice competition between lovers who are angry at each other.

"I'm angry," says one. "I'm going to twist this towel as angry as I am."

"You call that angry?" says the other. "I'm going to show you what angry is!"

3. Dance

Do a shaking, stomping, primitive dance. Pound your anger into the ground.

Ballet and most "artistic" dance won't do here. Such dancing is too refined, demands that dancers concentrate on their bodies instead of on their feelings and on pushing their feelings out through the body.

I am often asked whether sports help release anger. My answer is the same as the one I've just given for dance: Any form of exercise will release anger *if* the exercise is consciously done with that end in mind. If you're angry and go for a five-mile run but you don't focus your running on the anger and you don't consciously *express* *it* in the pounding of your legs and perhaps in groans and yells and sobs, then no, it won't do much good. You'll have a nice workout and be tired, but you won't be less angry.

But if you say, "I'm going to run this anger out, squash it into the earth, snarl, and make faces till I feel better," and you keep thinking and doing this as you run, you will discharge your anger.

The same holds true for hitting a racquetball or tennis ball against a backboard or throwing a ball against a wall: Unless you consciously use the activity to express your anger, it's just a physical workout.

You have to say, "I'm going to hit this ball as hard as I can and say how angry I am about the stuff that happened on the job today." And then you have to *do* it, grunting like Jimmy Connors or Monica Seles, until you've used your angry energy up.

If you swim, hop into a pool or pond, and run and shadowbox and scream underwater. One of my former clients tells me he shouts and sobs his angers and griefs out underwater while he's swimming laps.

If exercising outdoors is a problem for you, you can buy a round Nerf ball and throw it against your bedroom wall without damaging anything.

How about competitive sports—do they get rid of pent-up anger? Not for most people. Those sports aren't undertaken for this purpose, and in doing them, anger is often *cultivated,* husbanded, not released. After a football or basketball or hockey game, many athletes are as angry as they were before—maybe angrier, because they've taken cuts, hits, and bruises and, like as not, lost.

4. Beat a Drum

Get a drum and pound on it.

The drum should be made of wood and animal skin, and you should pound with your hands, not with sticks. Big drums are better because you play them against your body, often between your knees, and their sound resonates deeper into you. Playing any kind of musical instrument can be helpful, as can singing.

Again, though, you have to concentrate on the reason you're doing what you're doing: You're angry, and you're putting your anger into the noise you're making. When I'm drumming I often make as much noise yelling and growling and groaning as the drum does.

Exercises 1 through 4 are all nonviolent, and they may not be vigorous enough to release your deepest anger and rage. I will come to more intense exercises in a moment.

First, I want to tell you an energetic and very nurturing exercise you can do if you're not angry but someone you love is. If your ten-

or twelve- or fourteen-year-old son or daughter is angry and you want to show them their anger's okay, consider doing the following:

Take off any rings you're wearing. Put your index and middle fingers together, holding them straight, side by side. Offer those fingers to your child, saying something like, "Hon, I know you're real angry now. It's perfectly all right for you to be angry. Your emotions are always fine, and I want you to know I support you in what you're feeling. If you want to, I'd like you to squeeze my two fingers as hard as you are angry. It won't hurt me a bit, so long as you squeeze and don't twist."

Your children may not squeeze your fingers the first time you make the offer, but they may during a subsequent anger. In any case, they will see that it is now okay to feel angry, as perhaps it wasn't when they were younger. They will see that you want to be with them in their anger—that you don't want to lose touch even *then*.

This exercise is perfectly safe. I have done it with hundreds of people. If the index and middle fingers are grasped and squeezed straight, there is no pain whatever.

If you have any pain, you're doing it wrong! Stop and reset your fingers. While your child squeezes your fingers, be sure to keep taking big, deep breaths so you won't take in his or her anger.

This exercise helps remove anger from the arms, hands, shoulders, and neck of the people doing the squeezing. More important, it shows them how important they and their feelings are to you and that you can be with them in their anger because their anger is okay.

If your spouse or lover is angry at someone or something other than you, offer to do this exercise with him or her.

MORE INTENSE PHYSICAL EXERCISES

I am going to speak now about exercises that use extreme physical force. A few of these exercises do damage to inanimate things, but none of them does the slightest harm to any person, either exerciser or bystander. You will use these exercises when your anger is so strong that you almost can't hold it in: Your body is racing, your jaw is clenched, your head bobs up and down, your hands claw the air. When you need exercises like these to discharge your feelings, you are dealing with suppressed anger of great depth.

1. Punch a Pillow

Punch a pillow—or a punching bag. And while you do it, yell and curse and moan and holler. The sounds you let out are very important, because they help articulate the preverbal anger and pain you carry from deep in your childhood.

Punch with all the frenzy you can. If you are angry at a particular person, imagine his or her face on the pillow or the punching bag, and vent your rage physically and verbally. This will feel contrary to all the "decent" ways of behaving you've been taught: to hit the imagined face of a relative—your father, mother, sibling, uncle, aunt, grandparent, cousin—or friend, and hit it furiously, constantly, as hard and fast as you can, all the while screaming your hatred at the person. You will feel as if you are betraying the relative or friend.

In fact, though, the real betrayal happened long ago, when the person wronged you or left you or disappointed you, a helpless child who knew only that you had to be loved and accepted. You will be doing violence to a pillow or a punching bag so that you can stop doing violence to yourself by holding in poisonous anger and hatred.

You are not hitting a person. You are hitting the *ghost* of that person—a ghost from the past, a ghost alive in you that must be exorcised in a concrete, physical way. You need to beat this devil out of you because, if you don't, your anger is such that you might possibly hit a real person in present time. Which would be *real* violence.

In our culture, women are discouraged from expressing aggression, and many of them find it difficult to hit and kick things. *The New York Times* recently ran a sports article about women who "boxercise"—punch punching bags for exercise. One of the women, Lisa Polansky, forty-one, said, "I can't believe I like boxing, because it goes against so many things I believe in. But I really like it. I think a lot of women grow up thinking hitting is wrong, it's bad. At first I wouldn't hit the bag as hard as I could: 'Girls don't do that.' It was hard to hit with a vengeance, really hard. But now I can picture a situation, get angry, and do something about it.'' She gets it out of her system by hitting something safe as fiercely as she can.

When I suggest pillow-pounding or couch-kicking to people in anger workshops, occasionally a man will say, "Look, John, I'm mad as hell. I don't want to hit a pillow—I want to hit something hard! I want to smash my fist into a wall! Or kick a boulder with my bare foot!'' Such a response shows the tendency toward self-destruction that's strong in angry people. What the man is saying is, ''I'm tremendously angry and the person I'm angry at is me. Hitting this wall feels right because it hurts me.''

In our fury we have all done stupid, self-punishing things. I remember bloodying my fist against a tree and kicking a fire hydrant so hard I limped for days afterward. I don't want you to make the same mistakes. This book is setting forth *healthy* ways of dealing with anger. I want you to be able to express your anger so that *nobody* is hurt, least of all you.

2. Break Glass

Break glass. Smash plates. Pound nails. Chop wood. Tear up phone directories.

And while you do these things, concentrate on your anger and on forcing it up into your arms and torso and mouth and face, so that you can expel it into the world.

A former client of mine goes to garage sales in his neighborhood, buys up twenty-five-cent dishware, carts it home, and stores it until he feels enraged about something. Then he hurls the dishware, piece by piece, against a limestone wall away from people. He turns a beach-blaster up loud so he can shout if he wants to. In ten minutes he's finished.

The difference between smashing your hand on a wall and smashing a plate is more than just the fact that the former hurts and the latter doesn't. Smashing your hand is *self-directed* anger. It points your energy back into yourself. I have already spoken about why self-directed anger is dangerous and almost always misguided. Smashing plates or tearing up newspapers or punching pillows—in short, discharging physical tension into inanimate things—moves your anger out of yourself into the world.

3. Go Outdoors

The outdoors is a great place to express your anger. Get out in the woods. Throw rocks. Beat branches against the ground or a boulder or a dead tree. Behave like a savage—you're trying to push the savage in you up to the surface and out. Yell like Tarzan. Bray like a mule.

When you're finished, you'll feel more serene, relaxed, and at home in yourself. The savage in you having been eliminated for the moment, you will be a person who feels no more than appropriate anger in an anger-producing situation.

CAN YOU EXPRESS YOUR ANGER PHYSICALLY BUT SAFELY WITH ANOTHER PERSON?

This is *very* hard to do.

I have heard of counselors who advise couples to express their anger toward each other by fighting with foam-rubber bats covered with fabric: Batakas, or Encounter Bats. The idea is that these bats don't hurt.

I totally disagree with this advice. Such bats *do* hurt. They sting on bare flesh. They can push into you in ways that hurt. And they are intimidating when someone stronger or angrier than you is clobbering and jabbing you with them. Two women friends use Encounter Bats on each other in Henry Jaglom's 1991 movie, *Eating,* and one of the women is plainly scared.

I am absolutely against expressing anger physically in ways that intimidate or hurt anyone. I am absolutely against violence toward people.

If you and your spouse or lover want to express your anger with each other, you have to agree on some ground rules first. Here are five I suggest:

1. Absolutely *no* physical contact, except as mentioned hereafter.
2. Absolutely no name-calling. No using the word *you.*
3. Each of you agrees to stay with the other so long as he or she releases anger in appropriate ways, and not to shame, laugh at, or humiliate the other person about his or her anger release then or thereafter.
4. Each of you agrees to honor the boundaries the other person sets. For example, if Russ says he doesn't want Sharon to come closer than five feet from him while he is releasing his anger, Sharon doesn't come closer.
5. Both of you agree to stop when either of you says, "Stop!" or "I want to stop."

Even with all these safeguards, I would suggest that couples begin with pillow-pounding or towel-twisting contests, where each does his or her own thing and there's no physical contact. Or cat-and-dog fights, where both snarl and shriek and yelp and bark and howl at each other, again without touching.

As for physical contact, I'd say:

1. Use the two-finger squeeze I explained on page 95. ("Squeeze my fingers just as hard as you are angry with me.")
2. Get six very soft, bulky throw pillows. Stand fifteen feet apart. Take turns throwing the pillows, one at a time, at each other. Say nothing more than "I'm angry!" and let fly. Grunt. If the pillows hit their target more than one time in five, you're too close. If the pillow hurts, it's too heavy.

Throw the pillows for a number of times specified beforehand or until you're tired by the exertion and, your anger discharged, reduced to laughter at the foolishness of what you're doing.

THE OBJECT, ONCE AGAIN...

... is to lose control safely. So that your angry energy is entirely engaged, enlisted, exercised, *used,* expressed, released, discharged, expelled, dissipated, used up, spent, depleted.

Not all people *can* lose control. Some of us are so mind-dominant that we need even more energetic exercises than I have described here to overcome our self-censor. There are safe exercises for such people, but they need to be done with an emotional-release facilitator or therapist in a controlled setting. I am not going to describe these exercises because they could be misused and hurt someone.

Let me make clear, though, that since the way to lose control is to overthrow the authority of our minds, we have to get out of our heads and, for as long as we can, entirely into our bodies.

If you're stuck in your mind, *move.* Get up from your desk. Fling your arms around. Throw a tantrum. Scream. Stomp. Twist and shout. Pound your mattress until you can't lift your arms anymore.

Generally, movement itself will bring up genuine feeling. If you don't get it by twisting a towel for five minutes, try ten. Or fifteen. And understand that the feeling you're going for may not turn out to be anger. You may twist a towel for ten minutes waiting to be furious, then find yourself weeping with frustration and disgust—and *that's* the emotion that needed to come up.

It happens all the time that a thin layer of anger, removed, exposes sadness, and people who started out raging finish in tears. They were sad and couldn't get to it for their anger.

AFTER THE RELEASE

After the physical release of anger, people feel better: happier, calmer, more energetic, more open. Ahhh! They sigh and breathe freely, their tensions gone. Often they feel even better two or three hours later than immediately after their release work.

If they are like me, they may find they want to talk with a safe person about what they learned from confronting their suppressed emotions. I call a close friend. ''Phew! I saw something I hadn't understood before,'' I tell him. ''I know why I did some things I won't have to do again.''

Or to Bev, my woman friend: ''I see now why I got so upset. And I apologize for trying to take it out on you. I can talk about the problem now without going crazy. Then we can make some healthy changes.''

7
People Who Can Help You with Anger-Release Work

Can you do anger-release work yourself?
I've already said, "Probably. Many people can."
Now let me complicate that answer.

YOU MAY *HAVE* TO DO THE WORK YOURSELF

Because you don't have the money to seek help. Or you live where help is unavailable.

But if you do the work yourself, you almost certainly will need the support of a safe person or safe people—friends, relatives, religious and lay advisers—who are able to listen to you talk about your innermost feelings without being hurt by what you say and without trying to hurt you because you said it.

If you don't have such safe people in your life, you must start looking for them. *One* such person makes the world a much sweeter place. Very few of us have more than two or three safe confidants at a time. We don't have the energy for more, which probably means we don't have the need for more.

How do you find such confidants? No one knows. Spiritual intimacy between people, which is what I am speaking of, is as much a matter of luck as love. In my experience, I'd speculate that most of us keep trying to build bridges to people whom we find sympathetic. When we discover, as we usually do, that the person we're drawn to isn't as sympathetic as we imagined, we withdraw, saying in our hearts, "Not him," or, "Not her," and, "Too bad," and, "That's life."

But we go on looking and starting new bridges. The problem is, those of us from dysfunctional families (which is to say, most of us) usually *long* to belong to other people. We move too quickly to make people confidants, mentors, lovers, spouses. We build our bridges too fast and pay too little attention to the signals we're getting from the other side. If we looked closer, we might see that the other person isn't really interested in us as we really are, but we're too excited by the possibility of intimacy to look closer.

We need to have the courage not only to build bridges but to build them *slowly*, little by little, trying out small confidences to see whether the other person is capable of accepting us as we are. If the other person isn't capable of doing this, we have to have the courage to admit it and retreat, perhaps dismantling the bridge. We have to have the courage to let go of people, even of *old* confidants, when we grow apart. Confidants are like lovers—they come and go. They are there for us at one time or on one issue and closed to us at other times or for other concerns.

I got a lot of support from a man friend in 1985 when I was grieving and raging over the wreck my parents made of my childhood. Four years later, when I was trying to stabilize my romantic life, the same man was no help. I'd talk to him, and he'd suck in his cheeks and frown.

"What do you *really* want to do?" he'd say.

A fine thing to say, except I saw he disapproved of what I really wanted to do. "He doesn't respect my wanting to settle down," I told myself. "He's happy playing the field. Maybe my wanting to settle down threatens him. Anyhow, he's not able to accept my feelings.''

I stopped talking with him about my love life. He's still my friend, but no longer a confidant.

If you're doing anger-release work yourself, you may or may not have a confidant, but in all likelihood you can find a group of people to hear you out nonjudgmentally while you talk about your feelings. That's what good twelve-step groups are for—Alcoholics Anonymous (AA), Adult Children of Alcoholics (ACoA), Al-Anon (for people in relation with chemically dependent people), Codependents Anonymous (CODA), Narcotics Anonymous, Gamblers Anonymous, Overeaters Anonymous, Sex and Love Addicts Anonymous, and the rest.

Now, it's true that not all twelve-step groups will feel safe to you, because, unfortunately, not all are. Some groups are shame-based and hence unable to support the expression of all feelings. You may have to start your *own* support group for anger sharing and anger release. If you do this, I recommend that all the group members be of your sex, at least to begin with. People have enough difficulty expressing their inner feelings to others of their own sex without the complication of doing so before members of the other sex. Men are taught that their anger will scare, and their tears disgust, women. Women are taught that expressing their anger and aggressiveness will make men think them unfeminine ''bitches.''

Groups must be run on the basis of the confidentiality of everything that happens during meetings and of empathetic support for members' appropriate and safe expression of their feelings. Groups should not follow the unhealthy 1960s confrontational model, in which members challenged what one another said and did and believed.

There are two great benefits to participating in a support group, twelve-step or other. The first is, you learn to tell the truth about exactly what you're feeling at the moment. The second is, you get to hear other people's feelings and problems, and their talk mirrors back your problems to you, so you see that other people are dealing with much the same stuff you are, that some have faced worse problems and come out fine, and that others are doing no better than you are and yet aren't ashamed to tell the group about their suffering and blunders.

A support group takes you into the fellowship of pain and healing and makes you see that, though you may have to do your emotional-release work by yourself—and in a sense we *all* have to, even if we have access to workshops and therapists—you don't have to do it *alone*.

WHY WORKSHOPS ARE HELPFUL

Whether or not you have done emotional-release work before, anger workshops—or support groups that encourage emotional expression—can be helpful in at least three ways.

First, they give you models of what emotional release looks like and show you that public expression of feeling can be done safely—that is, so that no one is hurt.

Second, they permit you to release your anger safely *with other people,* which, for most of us, is more beneficial than releasing anger in private.

Let's suppose you've never done anger work, were shamed as a child for expressing anger, and still believe that anger equals pain. If you go out into the woods and beat a branch against the ground, you will physically discharge your anger. This will feel very, very good.

But it won't heal your mistaken shame at being angry. It won't correct your mistaken belief that you are wrong to want to express your anger among people. It won't change your mistaken assumption that somebody will be hurt if you express your anger, because anger always brings on pain.

Your mistaken feelings would begin to be healed if you had done your anger release in a workshop with other people and seen that neither you nor they were hurt.

No one is hurt in an emotional-release workshop or support group because no one directs their anger at anyone present. As a child, you wanted to direct your anger at your parents, were crushingly punished for it, and learned to hide, swallow, and suppress your anger *in all situations*. You bring from your childhood the gut feeling that anger is too unsafe to be expressed around people. The workshop or support group shows you different—shows that done properly, in an appropriate situation, the expression of anger harms no one and indeed can actually bring people closer.

To express your anger in a way that's healthy, you've got to feel safe. If you feel safe doing it only when you're by yourself, the part of you that's scared of other people isn't being healed. The workshop gives you, who were hurt among other people, a chance to start healing among them.

The third way an anger workshop can help is that it has a facilitator to help you get in touch with your anger and express it.

I am an anger or emotional-release facilitator. I'm not a therapist, though I have trained hundreds. I have a great respect for therapists. I create a safe, caring, supportive, blame- and shame-free environment where people can feel their feelings and physically express them.

I got into facilitating emotional-release work because, as I told you earlier, I benefited from it so much myself.

Facilitators and therapists who have done their own emotional-release work can help you over the dozen barriers that keep you from expressing your anger and grief. Help you past "politeness" and "decency" and "good taste" and the religions telling you that "violence" is bad and the social stereotypes telling you that men don't cry and women don't get angry. Help you past the "shame" of making a spectacle of yourself and the fear you'll fall irrecoverably to pieces if you let go.

Facilitators in workshops are able to call on experienced or extroverted people to do the release work ahead of the people who are new or shyer, so that the new people can see how the work is done and that no one is hurt, no one has a heart attack. That way, the new people are more encouraged to try it themselves.

Furthermore, though only a small number of the people at a workshop may do an emotional-release exercise, everybody there benefits from the session. An exerciser gets to his or her anger, feels, and expresses it until, "Ahhh!" it is released; everyone watching has the vicarious experience of the catharsis. The exerciser's struggling and working hard and finally feeling better makes those watching feel better and feel that there's a point in *their* doing the same thing.

THERAPISTS

Therapists are useful for people who are head-centered; who come from controlling, often religious backgrounds; and who have in them a great deal of suppressed anger around which they have constructed elaborate systems of denial so that often they honestly *don't know* they are angry.

Denial is tricky. When you're in it, you don't know it; if you *could* know it, you wouldn't be in it. Denial is the ultimate method of suppressing feeling. It is very hard to overcome. Psychologists estimate that maybe 40 percent of all clients end psychotherapy still in denial—their psychotherapist unable to crack their shell.

My strong suspicion is that you don't need to worry much about denial. If you've read *Facing the Fire* this far, what I'm saying speaks to something in you. That something in you knows you are angry.

That something in you is almost certainly your child-self, which was so abused in your early years that it went into hiding. To regain some of the joy, energy, and spontaneity of your child-self, you have to let it discharge its lifelong fury and grief at the cruelty that shut it down.

Can a therapist help you do this?

Yes, of course—the *right* therapist can.

Who is the right therapist for you?

First off, whether you're doing emotional-release work or traditional psychotherapy, the right therapist for you is someone you like. It doesn't matter what the man or woman's specialty is—Freudian, Jungian, cognitive, Gestalt, bioenergetics, Rogerian, addiction, primal scream. What matters is that you feel safe and good with that person. Try a therapist for a session or two. If you don't feel rapport, try another. And another. And another. Don't worry that you will hurt a therapist's feelings if you decide not to work with him or her, or when you decide to stop working. The therapist is your employee, there to help you.

If you want to do emotional-release work, the right therapist for you is someone you like who has dealt with his or her own anger and grief. I strongly believe that clients can't go further than their therapists have gone. The therapists themselves may not have done formal emotional-release work, but they have faced their own denial and overcome the thousands of mental tricks we play to keep from feeling what's at our core. The best therapists know exercises and strategies and techniques for making you feel comfortable about coming into touch with and expressing your feelings, and they will adapt those devices to your individual needs.

How can you tell whether a therapist has dealt with his or her suppressed emotions? You can ask. If the therapist is a traditionalist, he or she won't tell you—will say something like, "We're here to talk about you, not about me." To which you have a perfect right to reply, "All right, I won't ask about you. I'll put the question in general terms. What do you *think* about anger? Do you think it's in the body? If so, how do you think people get it out?" If the therapist isn't willing to answer these questions, or if you're not satisfied with the answers you get, I'd suggest you find another therapist.

The emotional-release work I'm advocating is closest to the ideas put forth in bioenergetics, Gestalt, psychodrama, neo-Reichian, re-evaluation counseling, primal scream, and Hakomi therapy. But this doesn't mean that all specialists in these fields have dealt with their suppressed emotions. Nor does it mean that specialists in the other fields *haven't* dealt with their suppressed emotions. For example, though Freudian and Jungian thought do not discuss the body in the same ways we have been talking about, some eclectic Freudian and Jungian therapists have not only understood but felt and released their buried emotions.

You have to judge each therapist as an individual. What you are looking for is a therapist who is not afraid of feelings—his or her own, or yours. And I must tell you, from what I've observed, that such therapists are rare. If a client goes to a therapist and says, "I have a lot of anger about my mother or my ex-husband, and I want to work on it," the traditional therapist won't know what to do. He or she may not even know what the client means. The traditional therapist will say, "Okay, let's talk about that"—which is a fine thing to say—and start gathering background information, which is a necessary thing to do, but which need take only a couple of sessions. The therapist will go on gathering background information for weeks and months, never stopping except to say, "Tell me about that," or, "What do you feel right now?"

After six months of consultation, the client is likely to be steaming with rage or 100 percent in his head. He probably won't be enough in touch with his body to say, "Look, I came here to deal with my anger, and you've got me talking about this and that, and I still haven't got my anger out." (If he did say it, the therapist would reply, "Okay, let's talk about that.")

Most therapists find it difficult to deal with an angry client because they aren't trained in emotional-release work and, more important, are scared of anger—as everybody is until they learn better. When a client says, "I'm angry with my father and I want to let it out," a therapist has to be comfortable with his or her own anger—which means, has to have dealt with it in the past—or the therapist will, consciously or not, steer the client away from the emotion.

Most therapists are frightened of emotion, *any* emotion, "positive" or "negative." That is why they became therapists: so they could *understand* emotions and not have to feel them. Most therapists are— to borrow a term from the 1960s—control freaks. They come from dysfunctional families and use the therapeutic environment and their specialization as a shield against disorder and irrational behavior. They particularly fear and avoid anger for the same reason most of us do: Their history makes them think anger always brings on pain. They don't allow the client to express his or her anger because they are in denial about their own, and someone else expressing anger would risk resurrecting their own from the grave of their body, where it's buried.

A good many therapists, like the psychiatrist I was going to when I started with Dan Jones, have dealt with their own grief but not with their anger. Being comfortable with grief, they guide their clients away from anger and into grief. Grief is of course a more inward-pointing emotion than anger; it seems "safer," more manageable. Furthermore, grief has a measure of psychological respectability because Freud, the founder of psychotherapy, was riddled with it and made a grieving view of the human condition the basis of what he called the "reality principle." (In a characteristically resonant and gloomy sentence, Freud wrote, "Life, as it is imposed upon us, is too hard for us; it brings us too many pains, disappointments, in-soluble tasks.")

When a client starts to explore her buried anger, these therapists encourage her to grieve instead and support her crying. They may even tell her that crying will discharge her anger, because anger is a "secondary" emotion, the basic emotion being grief or sadness. This is, of course, untrue. Anger and grief are equally "basic" emotions. As I've said, they are often intertwined, even simultaneous, but they both have to be dealt with.

As I've said also, most men have more trouble getting to their sadness, and most women more trouble getting to their anger. This is in large part a consequence of upbringing: boys are shamed for crying, girls for aggressiveness; boys are praised for being aggressive on the sports or battlefield, girls are hugged for crying. In my experience, many women (and some men) cry when they're angry not because they're angry but because they are sad and frustrated that they can't *get* angry. They couldn't get angry as a child because it wasn't "ladylike," and they were expected to be a "good little girl" (or boy) or be punished. These women can't get angry now because the men they've lived with for twenty years won't support them in their anger and expect them always to be bright and cheery.

Such women—and some men too—may not even realize they are angry. They may get stuck in their sadness and consequently stuck in their lives, because sadness doesn't get us out of a stuck situation nearly as fast as anger. To be metaphorical for a moment, such people may pour the water of their tears on their anger and, the fire in them drowned, turn old before their time.

Sadness and anger should go hand in hand. When people are doing anger work and start crying, I support their tears. But I say something like, "Let the tears come, but not at the expense of your anger. Because tears won't get rid of the anger. Put them together if you want to, but don't do one in place of the other just because you're afraid to go further with the anger and it's okay to go further with the tears."

Many people need help doing emotional-release work. My own feeling is that workshops and group therapy provide the best help because you see other people doing the work, and you see that it's safe before you do it. If workshops and groups don't work for you, though, and you can't get in touch with your emotions on your own, try a therapist. The person you need may not be easy to find, but he or she exists, I promise. Be persistent.

IV
Your Anger and Other People

To this point, the purpose of my book has been to help you get your anger out in ways that don't hurt you or anyone else. I've recommended that you physically express your anger from your body while you are not in the presence of the people at whom you feel you're angry.

From here on, my purpose is to help you express your anger appropriately toward other people *in their presence*.

Before you do this, you have to know two things:

1. Your anger toward this person or these people is caused by your present situation with them and not by past emotions you've suppressed.
2. You are safe expressing your anger with them. Those are the subjects of our next two chapters.

8
Checking Up on Your Anger

How can you know whether your anger is present or suppressed? Immediate or buried? Appropriate or misplaced? Even more basic, how can you know how angry you are?

I've already suggested the answer: You can check your body. Your body is a sure barometer of your feelings. Pay attention to what it's telling you.

Most people don't pay attention to their bodies until they fall sick. That's a big mistake because your body—something you always have with you, as Groucho Marx used to say—is the only thing in the world that, if you observe it closely, always tells you the truth.

The truth your body tells may change from moment to moment because you have mixed feelings about something. That's normal—and it shows that your body is faithfully reporting every nuance of your emotion.

Imagine how many bad marriages could have been avoided if people had had the courage to pay attention to their bodies saying, "No, no, no, wrong, wrong, mistake! It won't work, I feel sick," on wedding-day morning.

Your body is where you are, what you are, and who you are at every moment. The way to know where, what, and who you are is to shut out the extraneous world and get into your body. The easiest ways to do this, as I've said, are through deep breathing and safely out-of-control activity: pounding pillows, stomping, screaming, twisting a towel, dancing, shadow-boxing. The choreographer Martha Graham used to say, "Movement never lies."

For years, girlfriends would ask me, "What are you feeling? Is anything wrong?"

And I'd say, "Nothing's wrong. I feel fine." I'd say it automatically. Without thinking about it. Whether or not I knew what I was feeling. Trying to protect them from whatever uneasiness was gnawing at me.

Now when I'm asked how I'm feeling, I say how I'm feeling. If I'm feeling uneasy, I say, "I'm feeling a little ragged around the edges," or, "I feel fair." My friends know my intention is always to feel considerably better than fair.

If I don't know what I'm feeling, I say I don't know. Then I may go off in a corner and do some yoga breathing or shut the door to my bedroom and take a tennis racket to the mattress till—phew!—my body can't do anymore.

When you don't know what you're feeling, you're often stuck in your head. As I've said, the quickest way to get unstuck is to *move:* to throw yourself around, jump, hit, kick, flail, shout, sing, pound. Agitate your body so much that your mind has to stop paying attention to itself and focus on your body and on what your body is telling it.

WHAT CAN YOUR BODY TELL YOU ABOUT YOUR ANGER?

Lots.

If your body tells you it's miffed, put out, annoyed, warm under the collar, you're probably angry about something that just happened. Your anger is probably present anger.

If, on the other hand, your body tells you it's steaming, shaking, outraged, beside itself, so furious it can't see straight or is seeing red, you're almost certainly *not* angry about something that just happened. This anger comes from the past, from your well of suppressed, unexpressed emotions.

You know what your body is feeling because your body tells you *and because your mind evaluates what your body says*. This is the point at which intellect and understanding intercede to protect you against doing anything unreasonable.

For example, let's say that Don, a paragon of dependability, is thirty minutes late picking up his wife, Peg, at work one day. When he arrives she's fidgety, tense, pacing the floor. She can hardly contain herself, and as soon as he walks through the door, she lets him know how she feels in words that almost blow him over with their force.

Let's assume the facts of the case are as simple as I've made them: Dependable Don is late one day, and Peg chews him out for it. Peg has overreacted. Her anger is about something other than being kept waiting that one day. An anger buried in her has been revived by something and has exploded outward.

Had Peg been mentally capable of reading her body, she would have known some past anger was at work in her precisely because her anger was so strong. She was so charged with angry energy that she could hardly contain it.

If you can contain a feeling fairly comfortably, most likely it has been stimulated by the present moment. If you can't contain a feeling easily, it's almost certainly caused by past events, people, and circumstances, and you're using a present occasion to release feelings you weren't able to release in the past because you would then have been punished, shamed, ridiculed, and—you feared—abandoned.

Uncontainable anger is almost always misplaced anger. Nearly all rage is misplaced anger.

I was driving on a country road a couple of years ago when a car pulled alongside, its motor roaring. The driver was shouting and gesturing at me. He gave me the finger and zoomed off.

"What's he so pissed about?" I said to my friend in the car. We'd been having a talk, and I suppose I'd been driving pretty slowly.

"It had nothing to do with you, John," my friend said. "Only a parent can make someone so mad."

I empathized with the yahoo giving me the finger, which is probably why I remember the incident. I myself get furious when somebody drives badly. When someone cuts me off, I feel like plowing my car into him. When somebody passes me going eighty-five, I hope at the very least he'll be arrested around the next bend.

I think I know the reason I get mad. It's because those "bad" drivers are getting away with something—breaking the law, making a mistake—and I feel that, as a child, I always had to be a "good" boy, was never allowed to get away with anything. "They're guilty! They should be punished!" I'm saying when I blow my horn or curse them.

The cliché is right: The people who make us angriest are those who show us things about ourselves we don't want to admit.

NOT ONLY IS UNCONTAINABLE ANGER USUALLY MISPLACED . . .

. . . *most* anger is.

When I was doing emotional-release facilitating for private clients, I saw a lot of angry people. In my experience, the people who are most angry are the recently divorced. They talk about their former spouses with hatred and loathing. Most of them jump at the chance to do anger work—particularly the women, which is a surprise because, as I've said, women are usually reluctant to show their aggressive emotions.

Divorce opens up a hole in people through which all their anger rushes out in a torrent. Much of the anger has little or nothing to do with the spouse from whom they have just detached. The spouse is the excuse, but they are angry at many other people: at the parent who most abandoned them, at the *other* parent for not protecting them, at the first boyfriend or girlfriend, at lovers, at former spouses, at children and stepchildren, at teachers, ministers, and nuns. They also feel more generalized anger—at having been oppressed, thwarted, and abandoned again and again in a variety of ways, and at themselves for having made bad choices.

Now, of course you have to deal with anger that's misplaced. *All* anger needs to be dealt with—expressed with the body and from the body. However misplaced or inappropriate, anger is never unimportant and can't be ignored.

If the anger called up by divorce is not expressed, it will recur with the *next* spouse. In the story about Peg and Don, an easy way to explain Peg's excessive anger is to imagine that dependable Don is her second husband. Her first husband, George, was so free spirited that Peg soon learned she couldn't depend on him for *anything*. She divorced him but never got her anger out. Five years later, when Don fails to pick her up, she's reminded of George's behavior and blows up at Don for things his predecessor did.

REALITY CHECKS

Checking your body will tell you how strong your anger is, and the strength of your anger will usually tell you whether the anger is present and appropriate, or past and misplaced. Before you express your anger toward other people in their presence, though, you need to run another check. You need to see, as well as you can, whether your anger makes "objective" sense.

When Bob got the note from Theodore, before he blew up he should have run a "reality check" to make sure that his fury was justified. He could have made such a check by phoning someone he really trusted, a close friend or counselor, and saying, "Here's what happened. I'm livid! Don't I have every right to be?" The friend or counselor would probably have responded like most dispassionate observers and told Bob his anger was excessive.

If Bob had made such a reality check and been convinced that his anger was excessive, *that would not have relieved him of his anger*. A reality check is a short-term intellectual escape and does nothing to discharge anger. To express his anger appropriately, Bob would need to do emotional-release work of the kind I've described.

Those of us who come from unhealthy family backgrounds need to do a lot of reality checking with clear-headed people because much of the time we don't know what sensible behavior is. Once we learn—and, thank God, we *can* learn—we can do a good deal of our reality checking by ourself. That is what Ellen did when she got Edgar's note. She ran her own reality check and saw that she had no reason to express to Edgar the anger she felt. If she still had that angry energy at the end of the day, she'd take it out in exercise or screaming in the car.

We have just seen that reality checking can be done both introspectively and with people not involved in the conflict. Can it be done directly with the person you're angry with? Could Bob do it with Theodore, or Ellen with Edgar?

Yes. In fact, as you may remember, Ellen plans to do it with Edgar as soon as he returns. She's going to ask him why he's dissatisfied with the report she drafted. She might begin, "I have the feeling you're annoyed with the report I wrote. If you are, for heaven's sake tell me why."

If a relationship is healthy—that is, if it is built on truth and trust—people can tell each other anything, even express their anger with each other. People in a healthy relationship don't have to guess at what the other person is feeling: They can flat out *ask*.

9
Feeling Safe

Getting rid of your anger, becoming who you really are, being more intimate with people you care about—these all begin with feeling safe. To experience and express anger, you have to feel safe, whether you're alone or with other people.

If you don't feel safe experiencing and expressing anger when you're alone, it's probably because you are imagining other people in the room with you. You imagine your mother or father, your spouse or friend, your teacher or child suddenly there in the doorway, saying, "Why are you hitting a pillow? And howling? How can you *do* that? Aren't you ashamed?"

If you don't feel safe experiencing your anger in the presence of other people, it's because you're concerned about what they will think, how you look, how they are going to judge you, whether you will be abandoned. We have said that the way to get rid of anger or other suppressed emotional energy is to lose control safely. Obviously you can't do this if you're not feeling safe.

If you're with people whom you feel are unsafe, you won't be able to express your anger to them straightforwardly or fully. No matter how appropriate, reasonable, and justified your anger is, no matter how deeply you feel it, you'll do all you can to keep it in—as, I would argue, you *should* do—because unsafe people will be hurt or enraged by your anger and will try to hurt you for it.

WHO IS UNSAFE?

A sizable minority of the population are *clinically* unsafe to be around. They are mentally deranged, alcoholic, drug addicted, or given to physically abusing others or themselves. If you are angry at someone who has any of these characteristics, you aren't safe expressing your anger to them. Such people can't control what they do.

But these aren't the only unsafe people. If you are angry at people who are vindictive or withholding or haughty or bitter, or dependent and clinging and fragile, you are also likely not to feel safe. Such people will try to punish you, if only by making you feel guilty, for expressing your anger.

If you don't feel safe with someone, you *aren't* safe. Feeling safe is largely a subjective condition.

Because it is, what makes *you* feel safe may not make *me* feel safe, and vice versa. Our bottom-line safety requirements may be— probably are—different. Some people can be with a vindictive person or a rager or a clinging withholder-of-approval/affection and still feel safe. Some people can be yelled at and called names or wept over and pleaded with and still feel safe. As I get stronger in myself, I find I can be with people when they're expressing stronger and stronger anger and not feel unsafe—so long as the anger isn't pointed at me.

For me, the bottom line for feeling safe is knowing that the person I'm with isn't going to reject, demean, ridicule, shame, abuse, or disapprove of me. If I feel people might do these things, I don't— *can't*—trust them. I don't show them my deepest feelings. I often don't tell them the whole truth. Why should I?

I'm being realistic. I'm saying what you know but may not want to admit:

- You can't love everybody.
- Most people prove themselves unworthy of your fullest confidence.
- There are many more unsafe people in the world than there are safe people.

Because our primary responsibility is to ourselves and our welfare, we have to be on our guard most of the time and with most people—because we aren't safe with them. To pretend otherwise is sentimental claptrap.

The problem, quite simply, is this: Most people believe that displaying emotion is a sign of weakness and that people who display emotion are untrustworthy. Few of us—but the number is growing—have learned the wisdom of General Norman Schwarzkopf, leader of the U.S. and Allied forces in the 1991 Gulf war, who said, "I don't trust a man who can't cry."

HOW WE CAN LEARN TO BE SAFE

If we grew up in an unsafe family, where emotions couldn't be expressed without people getting hurt, if we were shamed and blamed and ridiculed for what we felt, we have to learn what it feels like to feel our emotions and express them in a safe environment.

That's why psychotherapy and twelve-step and support groups that allow emotional release are so important. These are the first places where many of us can feel safe having our feelings. We are able to feel safe because the therapeutic setting and the example of other people enable us to stay in our bodies and *feel what feeling safe feels like*.

When we know what safety feels like—know it in the sense of having internalized it, taken it into our bodies—we begin to see how right we are to feel unsafe in the rest of our lives. The rest of our lives *is* unsafe.

TRUSTING OUR BODY

When we have experienced the way our body feels in safe circumstances, we know we can trust it to tell us when we are safe and when we are not.

Knowing this, we know the most important thing we need to know to be safe with other people: We know when to protect ourselves.

We know that if we don't feel safe with something somebody is doing, we can:

• tell them we disapprove
• tell them to stop
• stop them, or try to stop them
• leave

Of course, even when we have learned to trust what our body is feeling, we still are going to make mistakes about the people we trust and don't trust. Our feelings are infallible at the moment we experience them, but only for *us* and only for that moment. They are in fact totally irrational and powerless to foresee the future.

And people change. They seem one way at one time and another at another. Not only do other people change, *you* change; *I* change. We build bridges to other people and then decide we don't want to be linked to them. Love and intimacy come and go.

But though our feelings sometimes lead us into error, the fact remains they are our best guides to where we are at any given moment. Since this is the case:

If you don't feel safe expressing your anger or other emotions to someone else, don't do it. Go with your feelings.

If someone else is saying or doing something that doesn't feel safe and appropriate to you, don't stand for it. If you can't get it stopped, go with your feelings—scram.

MISREADING PEOPLE

I've just said we make mistakes about people. We have to, not being gods and having imperfect knowledge. Just because we feel someone is unsafe doesn't mean that person *is* unsafe. While I believe strongly that we have to rely on our feelings, I believe also that we must always be willing to analyze those feelings and see whether we can understand what causes them.

Sometimes we will find that our feelings about a present person are misled by that person's resemblance to someone in our past. If you feel someone is untrustworthy yet can point to nothing that person has done to justify your feelings, consider asking whether you may not be transferring—the psychologists' word is "projecting"—someone *else's* behavior onto that person.

You may find it helps to go so far as to make a list of how the present person reminds you of someone from your past ("Hank has brown hair and bushy eyebrows like Uncle Jake, who used to hit me") and how the two are different ("Hank is smaller than Jake, and I've never seen Hank hit anybody").

Analyzing our projections helps us to see present people more as they really are. Certainly if your therapist or counselor reminds you of someone from your past, you need to realize who and why and talk about this in your consultation. As Freud was the first to understand, making the unconscious conscious makes it more possible for us to live in the here and now.

FEELING SAFE WITH OTHER PEOPLE'S ANGER

In an anger workshop, when people do an exercise and get some of their anger out, I ask them, "How do you feel?"

They say, "I feel better."

They may say, "I feel tired." But they always add, "I feel better."

"Did you get hurt?" I ask.

The answer is always no.

"Did *I* get hurt?"

"No."

"Look around the room. Did anybody get hurt?"

"No."

They experienced and expressed anger, but no one was hurt. They learned that they don't have to be afraid of their anger or of letting it out in appropriate circumstances. And they learned that *other* people's anger doesn't have to hurt them and won't hurt them if the other people aren't trying to hurt or humiliate or judge them.

When people are safe, they can have their anger and express it, and the rest of us don't have to feel it, share it, or fix it. If we feel safe and healthy in ourselves, we can let other people have their feelings on their own, while we feel whatever we happen to feel at that moment.

We can even be with moderately unsafe people for a short period of time and not take in their emotions, if we keep breathing and checking our bodies and taking care of ourselves. Unfortunately, after a while the psychological ill health from which unsafe people suffer starts eroding the good health of those around them.

When people begin to get on my back, I feel it in my gut—a kind of queasy, slightly painful heaviness that tells me things aren't right in my world. As soon as I feel this, I tell the people I don't want to hear any more or to stop what they're doing. If they don't, I leave.

Because I know my bottom line: I have to feel safe. And to feel safe, I can't be attacked, browbeaten, condescended to, or called names.

Hell, I can't even be criticized. I feel that criticism is a weapon that unsafe people use to make themselves feel better by trying to control other people's behavior. Those of us from dysfunctional families grew up with endless criticism, and we internalized it to the deteriment of our adult health and happiness. We have got to learn *not* to listen to criticism, not even to our *internal* critic, that little ghost parent in us who keeps us from feeling safe and at peace. The following chapter argues my case against criticism.

10
No to Criticism

I don't believe in criticism. I don't believe in giving criticism—except in a roundabout way I'll explain in a moment—and I sure don't believe in taking it.

(Does this mean I never criticize anyone and never let myself be criticized? No. It means that not giving or taking criticism is the goal toward which I'm working. I'm a little further toward it than I used to be.)

GIVING CRITICISM

I don't believe in giving criticism because other people don't change until they're ready to. Until then, criticism—even "constructive" criticism, if such a thing exists—just makes them angry and defensive.

Say you're in a relationship with an alcoholic. "You drink too much, Gregg," you tell him. "You make a spectacle of yourself. Aren't you ashamed?" Pure criticism. And Gregg's response is likely to be a punch in the jaw for you, or drunken tears on your shoulder.

We don't have any business criticizing people this way. When you say, "You drink too much," you're saying, "I know what's better for you than you do." But there's no way you can know what's right for someone else because you're not that person. You're not his Higher Power (to use the Alcoholics Anonymous term). You're not God.

A BETTER WAY

You can make clear your opinion of Gregg's drinking without criticizing him. If we all used this way of relating to each other, the world would be a gentler, safer place. And we'd all be able to express our anger in a way that doesn't attack, humiliate, or judge the other person.

Instead of talking to Gregg about himself, we'd talk to him about us. We'd talk about our feelings and relate those feelings to his behavior. For example, we might say, "When you drink as much as you do, Gregg, I feel scared. I'm afraid you may do something to your health. Or *my* health—like punch me. I get kind of sick at my stomach."

We haven't said a word criticizing Gregg. We have simply reported how we feel.

Everything we want to say to another person can be said in a nonjudgmental way simply by going inside and reporting what our feelings are. Reporting our reality. Not presuming to know anybody else's.

This "When you . . . , I feel . . ." formula is one of the techniques of safe, noncriticizing boundary drawing that I'll discuss in my chapter on appropriate ways of expressing anger toward other people.

TAKING CRITICISM

Equally damaging to a relationship is accepting someone else's criticism when you haven't asked for it. I recently decided I'm no longer going to be in a relationship with anyone who criticizes me.

A couple of years ago, after I'd published my first book, *The Flying Boy,* a man came up to me after a lecture and said, "John, I really liked your book, but I have a criticism."

"Oh," I said. "Yeah, what?" And I ducked my head and let him tell me.

It was a dumb criticism—something I'd answered in the book. But it made me feel crappy the rest of the day.

Back then, I was getting hundreds of letters thanking me, saying I'd helped, changed lives. Among those letters there would be one or two, unsigned, saying I was a dunce and charlatan and should jump in the lake. And I'd take those two letters more to heart than the other ninety-eight. It was sick.

So a couple of months ago, when a man came up after a lecture and said "I read *The Flying Boy, Book II,* John. I really liked it, but—" I said, "Stop right there. I'm glad you liked the book. But I don't want to hear what comes after that 'I liked it, but.' "

"Well," the man said, "there are some things in the book I didn't like."

"Well, I don't want to hear about them," I said.

He looked at me as though I'd spat on his shoe. "What do you mean you don't want to hear about them?"

"I refuse to listen to them. I don't have any room in my life for your critical comments."

"But you're a writer. You should want criticism so you can do better."

"Look, the book's published," I said. "Lots of people have read it. Some of them tell me they like it, and I appreciate that. Some of them say they don't like it, and I can live with that. There's nothing I can do about the book."

"Well, how about your next book?"

"If I want criticism, I'll ask people I trust to read it and say what they think. Gently. I don't want to be shamed. I was shamed enough as a child."

"Why," the man said, "that's just about the damnedest thing I ever heard!"

I felt good refusing to hear the man's criticisms. Having the strength to set that boundary was a testament to my taking better care of myself than I used to. There was a time when I would let anybody dump anything they wanted to on me. I felt like a garbage heap anyway, so that's where garbage belonged—on top of me.

If you want to say something nice about me, I'll listen all day long. If you want to say something bad about me, keep it to yourself. When I want "constructive" criticism, friendly suggestions, I'll ask for it. If I don't ask, I don't expect to get it, and if anybody tries to force it on me, I hope I'll have the presence of mind to say, "Stop."

We have all suffered too much from criticism, both giving it and getting it. Every time you criticize someone to their face, you diminish yourself—just as other people's criticism diminishes you.

The other day in a workshop a woman said, "I was talking to an old boyfriend for the first time in a long while, and he started criticizing me about a lot of old stuff. I told him, 'I don't want to hear this anymore. I've been made to feel defective all my life, and I won't allow it anymore.'

"My boyfriend said, 'People who love each other tell each other what they're doing wrong. They tell each other the truth.'

"I said, 'Horseshit! The people who love me don't tear me down. They tell me what they appreciate about me and keep their criticisms to themselves.' "

I wanted to cheer. That woman is 100 percent able to defend herself and her feelings from other people's inappropriate meddling.

Now, I'm not saying you can't get criticism if you want it and can't give it if the other person wants it. We're adults: We can do anything we consent to.

But let's be polite and *ask*. Say, for example:

"I'd really appreciate your honest criticism on this. I'd like you to be gentle, but if you can't be gentle, don't. I want the truth."

Or:

"I wonder if you'd be open to my offering a little criticism? If you're not, that's fine, and I appreciate your honesty. But there is something I'd like to say."

11
What to Do with Your (Present) Anger, I

Let's say you're angry with someone or angry about something specific. You've checked your body and perhaps also called a friend, and you're confident that what you're feeling is present anger of a force appropriate, not excessive, to its cause.

NOW WHAT?

Now you ask yourself whether your anger can be used to change anybody else's behavior.

As I've said, when you were an infant and expressed your outrage to your parents, you could sometimes change the world—bring a six-foot, two-hundred-pound person out of the dark to pick you up, hold and comfort you, change you, give you food. Then, somewhere in childhood, your feelings lost this power. Your furious complaints had no effect on the world's unfairness. You stopped expressing your anger because you found it no longer made people do what you wanted. Maybe you were punished, mocked, called a crybaby.

When anger didn't work, you probably went into your head to figure out some other way to get that two-hundred-pound person to do what you wanted or, at a minimum, accept you. "I'll dance for him," you told yourself, if you'd been admired for your dancing. "Or be a comedian. Or a good student. Or an athlete. Or cute and pretty. And then he'll pay attention to me."

But he—and she and they—still didn't pay attention to you, or not enough attention, so you went into your head to shut off the pain of not having been held enough, praised enough, played with enough, wholeheartedly *approved of* enough.

There was another reason you shut off your pain: because, if you didn't, you'd feel your anger, and you knew anger no longer worked. You'd internalized the message that good girls and boys didn't get angry without getting punished. You had learned that expressing anger didn't change anything.

I regret to say this is generally true.

TELLING OTHER PEOPLE WHAT YOU FEEL GENERALLY DOESN'T CHANGE THEM

In my anger workshops—every one, without exception—I hear the same thing:

"John, it doesn't do any good for me to express my anger. I get angry at my husband"—or wife or daughter or son or boss—"who's an alcoholic"—or a drug addict or a slob or sleeping around—"and it doesn't change a thing. I tell him how I feel, but I might as well be talking to a tree. He just keeps drinking. Telling my feelings is a waste of time."

"Yep," I say, "if you expect them to change anybody. If you expect your feelings to create change in another human being, you'll be disappointed 90 percent of the time. Maybe more."

Anyone who says that they'll teach you how to express what you feel in a way that will change other people, win friends and influence strangers, is misleading you. They are reinforcing the

infantile expectation that governed your behavior in the
that even then, when you were more appealing than you w.
ever be again, only worked some of the time. We all still have
deep in us an infant hunger to be embraced and comforted in our
pain and frustration. The vast majority of the time, the world doesn't
respond to this hunger.

If you're expressing your feelings to other people because you
expect to change the world, you are back again in your infant de-
pendency. You are almost certain to fail and feel a failure.

The Reason to Express Your Feelings to Other People

You express your feelings to other people not to change those people
or the world, but rather to change *you* and, often, *your relation* to
your world and the people in it.

Of the many good reasons for expressing your feelings to other
people, the best, I think, is so that you'll be able to say to yourself,
"Ahhh! I feel better. I was angry, and now it's gone. I felt my
feelings and expressed them to other people without shaming or
blaming them. Without a *breath* of criticism. I feel fine because for
once I told the absolute truth about what I need and want, and will
and won't accept. My husband"—or wife or child or boss—"is still
a jackass"—alcoholic, addict, unwashed hippie, petty tyrant—"and
five to ten million American children still go to bed hungry every
night, and the hamburger and orange juice interests are still tearing
down the Amazon rain forest, but I feel fine."

At the end of the book I'll talk about the serenity that follows the
appropriate expression of anger. (Serenity is just a lovely word for
the "Ahhh!" response I've spoken of.) At that time I'll also suggest
that the appropriate expression of anger to other people can increase
our intimacy with them.

Now, though, I want to spend some time qualifying what I've just
been saying.

Telling Other People What You Feel
May Change Them

It *does* happen. It happens very rarely. But it happens, and if your anger is present anger, you may decide to use it, indirectly, to try to change someone else's behavior.

Here's what you do:

- You express your anger to another person or other people in an appropriate way. (I'll discuss appropriate ways in the next chapter.)
- You establish and announce the boundaries of what you consider acceptable behavior. (I'll discuss this then too.)

Having done these things, you have changed your relation to the people around you and, through them, to the world. Your changes may cause the people around you to change.

An Example

A woman I knew grew up in a conservative Christian home where she was taught that men were superior to women and that anger was of the Devil. She didn't read Dostoyevski, but she would have agreed with him that true followers of Christ ask not that their burdens be made lighter but rather that they be allowed to take on the burdens of other people.

This woman, who had an alcoholic father, married an alcoholic. The woman suppressed her anger, retired to her bedroom, wept, and prayed that her husband would stop drinking. She prayed to Jesus that He would intervene and make her husband become the man she knew he really wanted to be. She began her prayers, "Come on, Lord Jesus," as though Jesus were a competitor in a sports event— a horse race, say.

Jesus lost the race. Her husband kept drinking. He would say he was going to stop. He would sometimes weep over his shortcomings, excoriate himself, beg her forgiveness, and promise to become the man he knew she wanted him to be. But he kept drinking.

Years passed. They had three children. The woman never got angry. Not once. Had you asked her what she did with her anger, she would have said she didn't have any. If you insisted that she must, she might have said she was praying it away.

Though she never got angry, she got even. Through passive aggression, manipulation, sabotage, retreating, withholding, and illness, she showed her husband how she felt about him and their life together.

Years passed. She grew old before her time. The couple's children had variations on the problems their parents had. The oldest child, a son who had always been emotionally bound to his mother and to caring for her, started psychotherapy in his early thirties and then began attending AA and ACoA meetings. He did a lot of anger- and grief-release work. His example inspired his mother to go to Al-Anon and CODA meetings and to do emotional-release work with a therapist.

One Sunday morning, several months after she began therapy, the woman said something like this to her husband:

"You know I love you. I've proved it by staying with you all these years. I want you to do what you want to in every part of your life. If you really want to keep on drinking, that's what I want you to do.

"But if you want to stay with me, as I hope and pray you do, you can't keep drinking. This has gone on long enough, and now, for my own happiness and well-being, it is going to stop or you are going to move out.

"I know stopping won't be easy, but there are people who can help you stop if you want to. I will completely support you as you're doing it. If you don't do it, you will have to move out, and then we'll see whether we want the marriage to continue."

The husband agreed to stop drinking, received medical and psychological treatment that enabled him to do so, and now attends AA regularly. He and his wife are together and happier than they ever have been.

I Know This Story Firsthand

The woman is my mother. Her alcoholic husband is my father. I am their oldest child, who was so bound to her.

Everything in the story is true except for the last paragraph. What actually happened when my mother said that she had had enough and that my father would have to stop drinking or get out is that my father kept drinking. He's still drinking today. My mother is happier than she has ever been. They are divorced.

I want to make several points about this story and my mother's experience.

The first is that the last paragraph I made up for the story *could* have been true. The alcoholic husband, faced with the choice of losing his wife or alcohol, might have chosen to give up alcohol. The and-they-lived-together-happier-than-ever ending sounds senti- mental, but endings like this happen all the time, have happened thousands of times.

The second thing I want to say is that my mother, though she waited thirty-five years longer than she should have to draw upon her anger, did so in a beautiful and heroic way. She did just the right thing. She gambled that stating her needs might bring my father around. When it didn't, she took the step she had to take in pursuit of her best interest.

She didn't lose the gamble. She *couldn't* lose it. True, she didn't entirely win. She couldn't achieve what she most wanted—life with my father sober—because that wasn't within her power; only my father could choose to give up alcohol. But simply by stating her needs and holding to them, she avoided what she knew she could no longer accept: life with my father drinking.

ANGER CAN CHANGE THE WORLD

It doesn't happen often, but it happens. When Candy Leightner's child was killed by a drunk driver, Leightner grieved, raged, and then focused her anger into the present-tense task of reducing the amount of alcohol-related carnage on America's roads. She founded Mothers Against Drunk Driving (MADD), the organization that is doing more than any other to encourage both "designated drivers" and severe punishment for drinking and driving.

Or consider Sarah Brady. When her husband, James Brady, Ronald Reagan's press secretary, was paralyzed by an assassin's bullet that was intended for the President, she translated her grief and fury into leading the effort to lobby Congress to restrict the sale of handguns. The Brady bill, which mandates a one-week wait before the purchase of a handgun, is a monument to James Brady's courageous suffering and Sarah Brady's courageous persistence.

Most of us can't be like Candy Leightner or Sarah Brady and use our anger to change the world. But we can be like my mother and use our anger to change *our* world.

Realizing, feeling, and expressing anger brought my mother the best life she's ever had. Don't tell her that anger is one of the seven deadly sins. In her case, being "good" and "Christian" were of tremendous harm.

How can anger help us in our relations with other people and the world? Let's make a little list:

1. Anger can get us unstuck from unhealthy behavior or relationships. Rage won't—but present anger can. Properly expressed, it can separate us from our parents in constructive ways. It can help us disconnect from relationships that have gone dead or that aren't good for us. It can empower us to burn the bridges of our dependence on other people and their standards, and on our society's hypocritical ideals, deadening stereotypes, and "realistic" assumptions (as, for example, that we have to tolerate drunk drivers and handguns for sale on demand).

2. Anger can drive us to protect ourselves against people and circumstances that hurt us. (Grief won't—grief is submissive.) Anger can strengthen our personal boundaries, embolden us to take command of our lives. When we got angry as children, we couldn't protect ourselves because we didn't have the physical, intellectual, and financial resources to compel others to respect our rights. Our anger was no use

to us—which is, again, the reason we learned to suppress it. Now that we're adults, our anger is supported by the full force of everything we are and have and know.

3. Anger can give us a lot of energy, and a different kind of energy than joy. Angry energy points outward from the body toward the world. Expressed anger can try to change things. Joy doesn't—joy embraces. (Rage doesn't—rage is either destructive or, like grief, submissive.)

4. Anger can separate us from the past. When we focus our anger on the person in our past who taught us a dysfunctional pattern of behavior, we begin to free ourselves of the compulsion to behave that way in the present. For years I was haunted by the fear that if I ever got angry at a woman, I would go for her throat, because I'd seen my father go for my mother's throat when I was a boy. Emotional-release work focusing on this event taught me, in my body, that I wasn't him and that I absolutely rejected his behavior. As long as I was suppressing my anger toward him, I was afraid I might do what he did. Now I know I won't. Anger freed me from the past.

5. Anger can give us self-esteem. Convince us, as my mother was convinced, that our happiness is worth fighting for because we deserve no less.

AND THERE'S A PERFECT FALLBACK

If your anger directed toward changing other people fails to do so, as it probably will, you still can go "Ahhh!" and tell yourself, "I feel fine. The shopgirl won't believe I gave her a twenty, not a ten; my spouse is addicted to wine coolers and *Wheel of Fortune;* our kids are out of control; my boss is total scum; the rain forest is burning; and I feel great. All the awful feeling is gone from my body."

12

What to Do with Your (Present) Anger, II

We begin this chapter where we began the last.

You are angry about something that somebody—call him or her J. Smith—has done or is doing. From checking your body and reality checking with a friend or counselor, you are confident your anger is appropriate to its cause, and you think that properly expressing your anger might possibly change Smith's behavior as well as make you feel better.

What do you say?

You probably don't know. For my first thirty-seven years I didn't know either. As a child, I wasn't allowed to express most of my emotions, anger chief among them, and I certainly never saw anger expressed safely and appropriately to another person. If you're from a dysfunctional family, you probably didn't either.

How then could we possibly know what to say? It's only because we *are* children of dysfunctional families that we feel we *ought* to know without having been shown. As is typical, we feel guilty about something that's not our fault.

There is a right and a wrong, an appropriate and an inappropriate way of expressing our anger and being truthful about it with someone else. We've talked about appropriate ways of getting in touch with our anger and expressing it, both alone and with uninvolved people (therapists, friends, support groups), but this is only part of managing anger. You need to know appropriate ways of expressing your anger to the people who you feel have caused the anger.

For me, learning to *speak my anger* so that the people involved in it could *hear* me took a whole lot of reeducation and practice. A lot of my learning, by the way, occurred in twelve-step meetings, among strangers, where I learned to communicate my feelings without hurting others and offer general advice without being critical.

In the remaining chapters of this book I offer you many samples of conversations that suggest healthy ways to speak your feelings, conversational strategies of a kind most of us didn't—couldn't—learn in our families of origin. My hope is that these bits of talk will convince you that you can tell safe and fairly safe people that you're angry at something they've done without jeopardizing your relation to them, and will show you how to do this.

You're angry at J. Smith. What do you say to him or her?

FIRST OFF, WHAT YOU *DON'T* SAY

You don't say, "Clumsy jerk."
   Or, "Some friend you are!"
   Or, "You disgust me."
   Or, "I hate you."
You don't name-call, blame, curse, shame, judge, demean, demoralize, ridicule, or even directly criticize Smith. Doing any of these things is an inappropriate expression of anger.

Since the 1960s, some counselors have advocated confrontational truth-telling: "Tell everybody what you think of them—to their face. Spill your guts. Don't worry what you say or how you say it. Just get it out." *I disagree* with this strategy. It is guaranteed to hurt other people and, more important, you.

At first, you don't even say "you" because it's too dangerous a word. If you're very angry, you can say, "Damn, I'm mad!" but not, "Damn, I'm mad at you!"

There are at least five reasons why you don't vilify Smith:

1. It is an inappropriate expression of the present anger you feel or claim to feel. You are not *that* angry at Smith. If you are, you *shouldn't be talking to him or her;* instead, you should be off somewhere working out your rage.
2. If you vilify Smith, Smith will hear only your hatred and abuse, not the changes you hope to bring about in his or her behavior. Smith will instantly become defensive and hostile, will shrivel up, withdraw, or attack.
3. If you use "fighting words," like ethnic slurs or derogatory names, you are likely to get a punch in the mouth. You don't want to get into a physical fight because you might get hurt, jailed, or sued.
4. You are likely, later, to regret vilifying Smith and to feel yourself the shame you tried to impose on him or her.
5. And most important: you are presumably not angry at Smith but *at something he or she has done.*

I say "presumably" because it seems unlikely to me that you could feel merely a present anger toward someone whose very being you despise. There are, alas, some of us capable of despising other people *in themselves.* If you find you despise certain people apart from the noxious things they do, you can't be "appropriately" angry with them. For heaven's sake, don't have anything to do with them.

The crucial distinction between expressing dislike of something a person does and expressing dislike of the person himself or herself was popularized by the psychologist Haim Ginott in his influential book on childrearing, *Between Parent and Child* (1965). He said that in disciplining a child a parent shouldn't comment on the child, only on what the child has done. Children should never feel that their self-worth is in question: They are good, though they may have said or done something bad.

The same is true, I believe, when you express your anger toward an adult person. The person shouldn't feel that they are being attacked, demeaned, laughed at, or discounted as a human being (as Jill Ker Conway felt when her parents punished her by pretending she didn't exist). The person should understand clearly that they are loved, or liked, or at least accepted, though you dislike something they have said or done.

WHAT *TO* SAY

The appropriate, the safest, and the most functional thing to say to the person you're angry at is, "I'm angry." "J. Smith, I'm angry."
Or, "Honey, I'm pissed off."
Or, "Mr. Gaines, I have to admit I'm annoyed."
Or, "Maria, I'm no longer good-humored about this."
Whatever you say can usefully be prefaced by assurances of endearment, like, "Honey, I love you," or, "Mr. Gaines, I like you as a boss and enjoy working here," or, "Maria, you know I consider you a friend."
Such assurances are strategic and optional. Your real message is *I'm angry,* period. *I'm angry,* end message.
Say, "I'm angry," and don't say anything else for a moment.

DON'T SAY ANYTHING ELSE FOR THREE REASONS

1. You need to check that you aren't angrier than you thought you were before you spoke. It often happens that when we begin expressing our anger to the person causing it, we open an old wound in us through which suppressed anger rushes, and all sorts of historical grievances and vilifying energies get mixed with our present anger.
When this happens, we are certain to say things we don't mean to say, *excessive* things we'll regret later, things other people won't,

can't understand—that will confuse, frustrate, and anger them and make us more angry.

If you find you're too charged with emotion to express your anger appropriately to a person who you now realize probably didn't cause most of it, apologize and tell the truth. Say something like, "I'm sorry. I thought I could talk about this without losing my cool, but I can't. I'm way too excited. I don't want to dump this anger on you—it may have nothing to do with you. I know I have to deal with these feelings, and I'm going to do it. When I get finished, I'll be glad to share my feelings with you, if it seems important at that time. Again, I apologize."

Or, "Honey, I love you, but I can't talk anymore. I have to do some emotional-release work." Or if that sounds too technical, say you have to do "soul work" or "get some things out of my system."

Having spoken, don't stay around to haggle or explain. Get away and do anger exercises and check out your feelings with a safe friend, a counselor, or a support group.

2. If you say nothing more than "I'm angry," the other person may short-circuit your need to say anything more. The other person will usually know why you are angry from the context, and he or she may speak up, apologizing. This avoids your having to rub salt in the wound and perhaps start a round of recriminations such as "I only did it because you did it first," and so on.

Anytime you say more than "I'm angry," you risk saying too much. When you say, "I'm angry," and nothing more, you are owning your feelings, which anyone with sense will accept. As soon as you make explanations for your anger, people start judging your reasons.

As children, most of us had to justify our feelings constantly to the big people in our lives. If we couldn't make a logical—and hence, unemotional—case for feeling as we felt, our feelings would be denied ("You don't feel sick. You just don't want to go to school"; "That doesn't hurt, a small cut like that"; "You don't need to go to the bathroom—you went ten minutes ago!").

But as I've said, feelings *aren't* logical: They just *are* (and they are *ours*). If we spend our energy explaining and justifying them and trying to make someone else accept them, we aren't *feeling* them; we are suppressing them while *thinking* of ways to win approval for what we ourselves, by our actions, are denying.

3. Saying "I'm angry" and nothing more gives you the opportunity to test whether you are safe with the other person. It may be that you have misread them and can't express your anger to them at this time, however appropriately, without their trying to hurt you, either by attacking you or by being hurt themselves. Their response to your appropriate expression of anger may be *in*appropriate.

If it is, *protect yourself.*

This is a really important point, which I want to expand upon here. It applies whenever you deal with unsafe people:

IF PEOPLE ARE INAPPROPRIATELY ANGRY WITH YOU...

... if they shout, shriek, curse, name-call, browbeat, rage, or weepingly accuse, don't put up with it.

Protect yourself. Tell them to stop. Say it commandingly: "Stop!" Say it louder than they are talking to you. Much louder, if your feelings—outrage, fear—require such a tone. If your saying "Stop!" stops them for a moment, say, "I won't listen to this. I won't be abused by you or anyone else. If you don't stop, I'm leaving."

If they don't stop, leave.

If they stop long enough for you to say something more, say, "If you tell me how you feel in an appropriate way, without trying to hurt me, I'll listen. Otherwise, I won't."

Inappropriately expressed anger is less a violation than physical force, but it is still a violation. *Don't stand for it.*

The more unsafe people are, the less you should argue with them. With really unsafe people, who are out of control or almost out of control, the best thing to do is to leave. Which is why, incidentally, it's so important for you to have dealt with your fear of abandonment: You're not free to express your anger toward others unless you're ready to give them up.

WITH SAFER PEOPLE

But let's say the person you're angry with is moderately safe, as—thank God—most people will be if your anger is present tense.

You say, "I'm angry," and the other person says something appropriate like, "Oh. Why?"

What do you do now?

Now things get much freer.

Now you can use dangerous words like "because" and "you."

I strongly recommend, however, that you rely less on these words than on words about your own emotions, using the "When you . . . , I feel . . . " formula to state your grievance at the other person's behavior.

As for instance:

"Honey, you know how much I love you. But when you leave your things all over the house, I feel put upon. Because I feel you're not doing your fair share of the housework, or you think I'm hired help."

"Margaret"—or Carlos or Mr. Gaines or Boss—"you must know how much I like you and like working on our project. But I have to tell you that I'm puzzled and more than a little annoyed by the decision you made to let Barbara go and keep Joe on. Everyone I've spoken with in the office feels Barbara was worth two Joes. When people have got to be let go, we'd certainly like the chance to give you our opinions."

"Son, you know how happy I am that you don't have my hangups about money. I come from a different generation, and because I do, I have stingy instincts. One of those instincts is that when people leave a house for the day, they turn off the air conditioner—which you forgot to do this morning. When I find it left on, I have to tell you, I start fuming inside, thinking of the cost. Maybe tie a string around your house key, so that when you're locking the door, you will ask yourself whether you turned the AC off."

"Sherry, when you tell me you're going to be here right at five thirty and you aren't, I get angry. So next time, just call and tell me you're held up, okay? There! I feel better for having said that. Phew, I'm okay now."

If you use the "When you . . . , I feel . . . " formula, nine out of ten people will be able to hear what you're saying without getting riled up. In my experience many will respond with something like, "I understand that," or, "I appreciate that," or, "I can hear you," or, "Right. I apologize."

The formula provides a gentle way of indirectly criticizing another person and directly stating your needs and wishes.

TAKING THINGS ONE STEP FURTHER

You have told another person that you are angry, and you have given the reason for it. You have suggested how you would like the other person to behave differently. The other person has heard you out and accepted your complaint.

In many cases—perhaps most—this will be enough for you, particularly if this is the first time you've aired the grievance or if the grievance isn't very important to you.

On the other hand, if the problem is important to you and is one you've spoken about before, you may have stronger feelings that you need to express. The first time, it was adequate for you to say, "I'm angry." After five times, it may be necessary for you to say, "I'm *real* angry now, and I want to tell you that."

Your next step, a drastic one, would be to restate your goal in contractual terms; "If you do/don't . . . , then I . . . "

This step does more than merely *state* what you want: it poses consequences if the other person fails to do what you want. This is what my mother did when she told my father, "If you don't give up drinking, I am going to insist you move out."

There is nothing gentle in this line-in-the-sand strategy, any more than there is in a loan-payment agreement that says that if you don't pay, we take your boat, car, and house, in that order.

Do You Draw a Line in the Sand? And If So, When?

You should take this step *only* if your feelings insist that you take it. If your body cries out for you to do it. I can't give you any rule of thumb here because you're the only expert on your feelings. The best I can do is tell you what you already know.

First, feelings come and go, so you want to check your feelings over time to be sure you hear all they're telling you. You do this through introspection, looking deep inside yourself, and asking what you feel now, and now, and now, and what you need at all those moments to feel good. You do this also by checking with your intimate friends, counselors, and support groups. Before making a decision, you discharge any anger or pain you have that might cloud your ability to know what you are feeling and to think things through. In short, you take care that your feelings are both clear and informed by the best "objective" thinking you can get.

Second, your feelings are yours, nobody else's. Friends, counselors, and support groups give their impressions of you and your feelings, but only you know what's at the heart of your heart.

Finally, learning to respect our emotions, follow our heart, *feel* our anger and grief is hard for many of us. My mother ran from her anger at my father for thirty-five years. I still find I have to discharge anger over things that happened to me fifteen, twenty, or thirty years ago. The ideal is to be so in touch with our emotions that we feel them when they happen, in the moment as we live it, rather than days or weeks later, to say nothing of years or decades. But most of us are far from the ideal and must be patient with ourselves and our slow reaction times, and feel out our emotions for as long as we need to until we know in our bones that we are reading them right.

Incidentally, if my experience is typical, the more anger we release from the past, the more likely we are to be in touch with our anger in the present and the quicker our response times get to be. If something made me angry in 1969, I probably felt it about 1984. Though I'm still having to deal with things that made me angry a generation ago, now when something makes me angry in time present, I usually feel it right away, or in a day or two at the most.

MATURITY AND CIVILITY

Those of us from alcoholic families have a warped picture of the world. We think in all-or-nothing terms. People are on the bus (or on the wagon), or they're off. Having been defenseless as children, we have now learned to protect our boundaries at all costs, including frequently resorting to the line-in-the-sand strategy (if you don't do so-and-so, you're off the bus).

Most people, including many from dysfunctional families, have a more balanced view of life and think in less black-and-white terms. And when we get strong enough to do so, this is the view we too should cultivate. For example, while we are waiting to be sure of what we feel about J. Smith, this person we are angry at, we should pay close attention to the reality of our relation to him or her.

Is it so bad?

You said, "I'm angry," and Smith responded well enough, safely enough that your conversation continued.

You told Smith why you were angry, and Smith didn't explode.

In fact, you each seemed to be taking care not to hurt the other. Maybe you can communicate with J. Smith better than you suppose.

How does Smith feel at this point about your expression of your anger? In a workshop, after someone has expressed his or her anger, I can ask them, "Were *you* hurt? . . . Was *I* hurt? . . . Was that person over there hurt? . . . Was anybody hurt?" It's hard to do this in life, but give it a try. Say to Smith, "Are you okay?"

Or, "You know, I'm afraid maybe I'm hurting you, and I don't mean to do that."

Or, "Do you want me to stop talking about this for now?"

It's always a good idea to recheck the sincerity of your own motives. Look inside yourself for a moment, evaluate your feelings. Can you honestly say, "I haven't shamed, blamed, ridiculed, demeaned, or judged this person"? Can you take in a bellyful of air and let it out in a big sigh "Ahhh!" and feel fine, not trembling sickly anywhere?

If so, your communication with Smith has been appropriate and functional from your point of view.

(If not, if you have tried to shame or blame, tell Smith you did this and apologize.)

I used to think that if one person expressed his or her anger appropriately to another person, there was no risk of the other person's being hurt. Unfortunately, this isn't true. I was wrong.

I should have remembered that not only are our feelings subjective, so are our impressions of reality. Rebecca can behave in a functional way, and Neal can see her as behaving dysfunctionally. Charles can express his anger appropriately to Janice, without meaning to blame or shame, while Janice can consider his behavior hurtful, demeaning, or judging.

Would this mean that Janice is unsafe? Maybe a little bit, on this issue, right now. But what matters is how she expresses her discomfort. Is her response to Charles "unsafe"? Excessive?

Let's say Charles has used the "When you . . . , I feel . . . " formula, and Janice responds, like a Woody Allen character, "God, I feel like you're *attacking* me."

To which Charles replies as to present anger (which is what Janice has expressed): "No, I wasn't attacking you. I feel fine with what I said. Keep telling me how you feel in an appropriate way so I can hear you."

Janice is upset, but she has voiced her upset in what I would consider an appropriate way, despite her slightly overemotional tone. She has talked about her own feelings and not vilified Charles.

To this point, Janice and Charles are not having a fight but a *civilized* argument—like those in a Woody Allen movie.

A civilized argument—the very term seems a self-contradiction to those of us who grew up scared to make our feelings known to Mom or Dad. We not only hate arguments, we want them *over* immediately because we're terrified that expressing anger is going to lead to loss of control and then to real pain. We have to learn that civilized argument is safe, that the people not to be trusted are those incapable of civilized argument. In 1972 the columnist Jack Newfield wrote a public letter announcing that he was not going to vote for Representative Bella Abzug because "I have seen her call too many good people 'cocksuckers'—and worse. . . . You cannot disagree with

Bella and have a human conversation.'' Newfield considered Abzug uncivilized or, in my terms, ''unsafe.''

Of course, a civilized argument can degenerate into a name-calling, even fist-throwing fight. Janice's insecurity may be so deep that she will start cursing or sobbing. In which case, Charles might say something like, ''Now, if you're open to a suggestion, maybe you're upset because what I said restimulated some old feelings of yours. If so, you need to take them away and deal with them.'' He may finally have to say, ''Well, we disagree, and I don't want to talk about it anymore,'' and break off the conversation. And leave.

In most cases, though, an argument that begins with an appropriate expression of anger will remain civilized. The crucial point to make is that, unlike the raging and shaming that took place in our childhoods, such appropriate arguing is safe, healthy, and potentially healing. It requires simply (!) that both sides have a measure of psychological maturity, that they express their feelings, points of view, and bottom-line requirements without disparaging the other side, and that they *listen* to the other side, without interrupting or attacking, and look for ways to accommodate the other's wishes without violating their own bottom-line principles.

When you appropriately express your anger to a safe or moderately safe person, you set up a framework for civilized debate, which may include argument. No one is going to be hurt in the debate, though they may of course be hurt by whatever result comes from it, as both my mother and father were hurt by the ending of their marriage over the issue of my father's drinking.

Your appropriate expression of your feelings to a safe or moderately safe person establishes the first level of intimacy between the two of you. The first level of intimacy occurs when both participants in a relationship *feel sure* the other person will try not to say or do anything to hurt them.

THE MAKINGS OF A CIVILIZED ARGUMENT: A SHORT LIST

What's appropriate behavior in an argument? What are the ground rules for fighting fair?

I suggest the following: both parties agree that:

1. There will be *no* physical contact.
2. There will be *no* name-calling.
3. There will be *no* shouting (unless both parties agree shouting is okay).
4. There will be *no* interrupting the other person's speaking.
5. All personal boundaries will be honored. (Thus, if Aida tells Fred to stay at least ten feet away from her, he does this.)
6. There will be *no* "looks that could kill," groans, or grimaces of disgust.
7. Neither party will walk out on the argument unless they feel unsafe.
8. They will take full deep breaths whenever they feel the need to express their anger.
9. They will (or will not) answer the telephone and doorbell.
10. Each person will do everything possible to make sure the emotion that brings him or her to the discussion is *present* anger and not anger from the past.

An Aside

Number 10 is crucial. *The reason most love relations fail is that one or both members of the couple have unmet childhood needs and unexpressed childhood anger.*

I'm going to get married, and I plan to have words like the following put into the vows:

Because I, John, love you, I promise that when I'm feeling anger that's at all strong about something you've said or done, I will take my emotion to a friend or therapist or support group before I discharge my feeling on you.

Because you love me, I expect you to do the same.

I expect us always to check out our anger at each other with a safe person or safe people to see whether the anger belongs to our relationship in the present moment.

When I have done this, I expect you to listen to me. If I haven't done it, I don't want you to.

When you have done this, I promise to listen to you. If you haven't done it, I don't want to.

CONCLUSION

Ten years ago I was afraid that if I expressed my anger to other people, I would hurt them or myself, or they would hurt me.

Now I am clear that when I express my anger appropriately to safe or moderately safe people, I will not hurt them or be hurt myself.

Most people find that anger that's appropriately expressed is easy to be around, once they get the hang of it and learn that (1) other people have an absolute right to feel whatever they're feeling and to express it as vehemently as they like so long as they don't use it to hurt anyone else, and that (2) anger doesn't have to lead to pain.

Appropriately expressed anger is a thousand times easier to be around than blaming or judgmental anger, of course. But it's also much easier than anger that's passive-aggressive, hidden, sideways, or seeping.

Inappropriately expressed anger, whether it comes from you or from other people, will leave you feeling drained and tired, as though something has been taken from you. As it has: your self-worth, energy, defenses.

Appropriately expressed anger, whether it's yours or someone else's, will reinforce your sense of who you are, where your boundaries are, and what you're responsible for and what you're definitely not responsible for.

13
Being What You Feel

You expressed your anger appropriately to the person who caused it. That person heard you and understood what you wanted of him or her. And then—nothing happened. Nothing changed.

No surprise in this. The world is unfair and unreasonable. People don't do what we want them to, even though we obviously know what's best for them.

You had the satisfaction of speaking your feelings and—"Ahhh!"—getting them out. But your feelings didn't change anything, as they usually don't.

What now?

Well, if you haven't already done so, you have to decide your next step. Ideally, you decided it before you expressed your anger and stated your needs. Presumably you didn't draw a line in the sand without knowing what you would do if someone stepped over.

If you did draw a line in the sand, you can now do your best to erase it. Let's say you said you'd throw your spouse out if he or she didn't stop drinking or leaving dirty clothes on the floor or putting the make on people at church, but your spouse continues to do what offends you. You can beat a retreat. You can say you've changed your mind, the offense isn't as important as you said, and you're happy to announce that due to Mother's Day and Father's Day both having twenty-four hours this year, you are offering your spouse One More Chance. Or two. Or more.

But do you want to do this?

Do you really want to keep living with an alcoholic, picking up after your husband, watching your wife sneaking off with deacons, getting nagged at a dozen times a day, soothing someone else's feelings, working for a company that pits employees against one another, sending your kids to a school that doesn't reward them for the things they're good at, hanging around people who don't care if they hurt you or who are so insensitive they hurt you without knowing it?

Maybe yes. Maybe no.

IT'S UP TO YOU

Your life is yours. You really are free to do what you feel is best for you. (You may think you aren't, but you are.)

And when you've done it and found you still haven't done the right thing, you are free to change your mind and try something else. You can always admit you've made a mistake and change your mind.

What stops you from doing this? Ninety-nine times out of one hundred, it's fear of what other people will think of you—fear, at bottom, of abandonment. (As we discussed earlier, an adult may feel abandoned, but it is the child in him or her who is feeling this. Remember: adults cannot be abandoned.)

In this chapter, I'm going to give you nine rules for being in relation with someone else and still living your own life. And then I'm going to make plain just how individual and subjective my definition of "appropriate behavior" is.

My emphasis on your *feeling what you feel* and *being whatever feels right* should not be understood to mean that if you feel like abusing, putting down, blaming, demeaning, demoralizing, ridiculing, judging, shaming, harming, or hurting people, you should do it. I am *not* suggesting this. To do any of these things, unless you are being viciously attacked, is inappropriate and dysfunctional. (Why dysfunctional? Because it impedes your communication with the other person. It gets the other person angry.)

Now, as I said in the last chapter, even if you avoid these destructive behaviors, other people may still be hurt by what you say or do, because feelings are subjective and other people are like you—free to feel whatever they feel. But if you have honestly avoided trying to hurt other people, *you are not responsible for what they feel.* Whatever they feel is their business. If they don't like feeling what they're feeling, that's their problem.

If they say, "You hurt me," or, "I feel you're judging me," you can say, "I'm sorry you feel that. Tell me about it in a way I can hear you. I have to tell you I feel fine about what I did. I may not always feel this way, but that's what I feel right now. If I can make a suggestion, maybe what I said reawakened some old pain of yours. If it did, maybe you need to take that pain somewhere and deal with it."

Of course, you may *not* have honestly tried to avoid hurting someone else—most of us spend a lot of time and energy putting other people down. If you did this and now want to try to repair your relation with that person, you need to make an apology. Tell the truth: "I'm sorry to say I did so-and-so because I *wanted* to hurt you. I regret this and apologize for it, and I assure you it's not what I want to do most of the time—like now, for instance. I consider you a close friend, and I hope you'll forgive me."

OKAY. NINE WAYS TO REMAIN YOURSELF WHEN YOU'RE WITH SOMEONE ELSE

1. Most important: Focus on yourself, not on the other person. Ask yourself, "What do I need now? What do I feel now? What do I want to do now?"

If you want to tell the other person the truth—which is to say, *your* truth—do it. Tell it. The other person is an adult. He or she will be able to handle it. If they can't handle it, that's their problem.

If you don't tell your truth, if you don't do what you feel like doing out of fear for how the other person may respond, you are stuck where you were as a child, having to pretend to be what you aren't so as to win your parents' approval.

When you ask yourself "What do I feel now?" you're really asking "What does my *body* feel?" That's a good question: Ask it of yourself. Then ask your body what it feels like doing. If what it feels like doing doesn't hurt you or anybody else, do it. Bellow, "Arrrrrgh!" Meaning, "I feel great!" Or, "I feel like crap!"

2. Don't fret about being "considerate" or "decent" with other people. Try to be functional—that is, try to keep the lines of communication open to those you want to communicate with, and to tell them what you want to say in a way they can hear without being hurt.

3. If you know people to be unsafe, don't have anything to do with them. Or as little as possible.

4. Don't count on people to appreciate your self-assertion or your having expressed your anger or other feelings, even if you've done so appropriately. People *may* appreciate it, but you have to expect they won't. If you count on them to validate your feelings, you're still a child in the infantile state of expressing feelings to change the world. And that's not why you're expressing your feelings. You're doing it for *you*—so *you* will feel better.

5. If you're worried about whether what you feel is "justified," remember: It's justified because you feel it.

6. Don't participate in someone else's pain or anger unless you really feel it. When someone is crying or raging, ask yourself, "Is this *my* pain?" If you don't feel it, it's not, and you don't have to take it on.

I remember how liberated I felt the first time I realized I could tell myself, when a woman was weeping in my arms, "Hey, that's *her* grief! I don't have to feel it. I don't have to do anything about it. I probably couldn't anyhow."

Do you think this cold of me? Do you think I should bow my head and suffer with my friends and lovers?

Not if I don't feel it. If I don't feel it but pretend I do, I'm just trying to look better in someone else's eyes, or make that person feel better. I'm caretaking someone else's feelings.

My responsibility to other people is to keep my relationships functional—that is, to be supportive. And when the other people are suffering, say things like, "You know how much I care about you. I'm sorry you're going through this, but you're handling it fine. You're letting yourself feel what you feel. That's great. I'd love to talk about it with you if you want to." Or, "I'm glad to sit with you while you go through this bad spot."

7. Don't second-guess what other people are thinking or feeling.

If you want to know, ask.

If they give you an answer, accept it.

If they don't give you an answer or if you don't believe the answer they give, say to yourself, "Okay. It's their problem. If they want me to know about it, they'll tell me."

8. If other people ask you what you're thinking or feeling, tell the truth if you can do so without scaring them or soliciting their pity.

A couple of winters ago I went back to my old stamping grounds in Alabama. While there I made a lunch date to see a woman I'd lived with and almost married. I arrived fifteen minutes early at the restaurant.

A middle-aged waitress smiled and asked me how I was, and I said to myself, "Now, if I were back in Austin, among friends, I could tell the truth—because I know they understand me. I don't know if this woman can." But she had a nice face, and I found myself saying, "Ma'am, I'm pretty darned scared. I'm going to meet a woman I loved and haven't seen in six or seven years."

The waitress chuckled and said, "Well, I guess I know how that is. Sounds like you need a drink."

"Well, no," I said. "It was my drinking made her call the whole thing off."

The waitress laughed and said that then she'd recommend something warm and comforting. We settled on cider, which she had heated up for me.

I remember how much better I felt, just having told someone the truth. I could breathe. I could be myself even with people I didn't know. I didn't *need* to be in Austin. I carried the real *me* wherever I went. I only needed to have the courage to bring it out whenever it might get a tolerant reception. If it didn't—if the other person turned out to be uninterested or unsafe—I had plenty of ways to protect myself. I had a lifetime of experience lying.

9. Don't hesitate to hate anyone who has hurt you. Whatever you feel is fine, including hatred, though you will be more comfortable when you work the hatred—which is simply frozen anger—out of your body.

WHATEVER YOU FEEL IS FINE...

...and this book is arguing that you should embrace what you're feeling at any given moment and express it in an appropriate way.

Expressing what you feel in an appropriate way, you will not mean to shame, blame, hurt, ridicule, judge, or embarrass other people, but this doesn't mean you will always obey our culture's guidelines for polite behavior.

If I am right, "appropriate" behavior can be individual and sub-jective—quite unlike "acceptable" behavior, which is established by social custom. If I am right, a person's behavior can be appropriate to him or her without being what the culture considers "polite," "decent," or "considerate."

If you are trying to express your emotions—notably such troubling emotions as grief, pain, and anger—and if you are unwilling to go beyond what "the culture" or "society" or "other people" approve of, you will fail. You might as well not have picked up this book, much less read all the way to page 160.

Because other people and our society are going to say, "Don't do anything upsetting. Be a good person, the way you've always been. Do what we taught you. Do what everyone else does.''

I know, because people tell me all the time that ''other people''—not they!—think that what I'm suggesting, the direct release of emotion, is dangerous, dysfunctional, disgusting, violent, absurd, and unhealthy.

Ask ten people whether they think screaming in a car or beating a couch is a good way to discharge anger. Nine of the ten will say it's sick. Indecent! That's why books like *Anger: The Misunderstood Emotion* and *The Dance of Anger* are popular—they don't fly in the face of our culture's norms. *Facing the Fire* is saying, ''Folks, the most important things we've been told about anger and the appropriate expression of anger are wrong—180 degrees off, downright pernicious. They go against human nature and the truth that lives in our body.''

YOUR ANGER IS YOURS...

... and the consequence of this is that there can't be any hard-and-fast rules about what's ''right'' and ''wrong'' or ''justified'' and ''excessive'' anger or behavior. You have to monitor your body, go *inside,* and feel what you're feeling at your heart's core, to know what's appropriate for you. You have to act in consonance with your emotions and the moment.

I'm not saying that shouting in the car, twisting a towel, pounding pillows, or any of the emotional-release techniques are good in themselves. I'm saying that for specific people at specific times they *may* be. Each of us should be working every minute toward the goal of *expressing* what we feel and thus actualizing ourselves.

I have sometimes said I can imagine a man so angry that it would be appropriate for him to pick up an ashtray and throw it through a window—*provided* that he knew no one would get hurt and that, afterward, he made apologies all around, paid for the broken window and any other damage he caused, and was willing to go to jail if the judge told him to. If there was a choice between throwing an ashtray or dying of apoplexy on the spot, who would not choose to throw the ashtray?

Anger is a physical energy, and it is a physical necessity to get this energy out of our bodies. Although we can usually hold in this energy, however strong it is, until we can discharge it away from other people, in some situations some of us can't wait.

Appropriate behavior in these rare instances is up to *the person who feels the anger*. That's the only possible standard. If Mary tries to obey Philip's rules of what is "justifiable" anger or what is the "correct," "polite," and "considerate" expression of that anger, then Mary has turned Philip into a parent, is attempting to regulate her feelings by his standards. And that, to me, is sickness.

RADICAL SUBJECTIVITY

I was led to see that appropriate behavior can sometimes be determined only subjectively by a family friend who suffered a physical disability. He had a bladder problem that occasionally forced him to urinate right away. If he didn't do it, he would wet his pants.

This man's work often required him to walk from one building to another through a small downtown park. As a teenager, I was with him in the park once when he abruptly walked to a tree and peed. I remember I was embarrassed and glanced around to see if anyone was looking. My friend noticed what I was doing and said, as he zipped his fly, "They've all seen it."

The police and the park regulars knew my friend, knew his problem, and accepted his behavior. They knew he had to act in a way that violated the social norms.

In some situations, circumstances may drive people to express their emotions in ways that are both appropriate and against normal standards.

An Example

Several years ago the woman I was with was chewing me out for not paying her enough attention. We were in a hotel, seated among a bunch of people. She was hissing at me.

She knew I didn't want to be criticized—certainly not for not taking care of women (I've done too much of that). Not, above all, when she and I had agreed many times in the past that the men she was really angry at for ignoring her were her ex-husband and her father.

I couldn't walk off or draw her aside because we were waiting for the airport limousine.

So I said, "I need you to stop it! Right now."

I could see she was embarrassed that the people around us had heard me. I had broken one of our society's rules of public conduct.

Later, she criticized me for this.

I said that what I had done felt appropriate to me. "I didn't shame you," I said. "I told you to stop it because you were trespassing my boundaries. But I didn't say, 'Stop it, you bitch!' Or, 'Stop nagging!' "

"John, you were practically yelling."

"I was angry, and I wanted you to stop. I suffered enough emotional abuse as a child that I'm not going to let anybody abuse me now for very long without stopping it. Which may mean backing up my words with a loud tone. That's my boundary."

"But everybody heard!"

"I don't care about them. I had to tell you I was angry and that you had to stop chewing me up. If ten men in business suits hear me and it bothers them, that's their problem. I and my feelings are more important than some people I don't even know. I'm not going to mold my behavior for them."

"What are they going to think?"

Did she really say that? I'm not sure. She knew me well enough to know that I was working like crazy not to give a damn what other people thought. Which is *hard* for those of us brought up to please other people.

When I said, "Stop it! Right now," I wasn't venting a suppressed rage. I was expressing a present-moment anger that I could have contained, though with difficulty. I didn't choose to contain it because I felt my anger was appropriate, and I saw no important reason to hold it in and every reason to get that yucky feeling out of my body.

I did speak louder than I had to. People heard me. I am sure some of these people were upset. I am also sure that some of them were indifferent and that some felt what I did was fine.

We have many cultures, or subcultures, in America. These subcultures have different standards for "polite" or "decent" behavior. Not all the subcultures are as tight-lipped as the Bible-belt subculture in which I was raised. Many, like the Mediterranean-American and African-American and Jewish-American subcultures, are passionate and emotionally expressive. And louder.

Most people from these subcultures are used to hearing emotions vehemently spoken. They would be less likely to see anything wrong in my "Stop it! Right now." (When I told this story in a workshop, a woman agreed, saying, "I'm Italian. In my family we shouted all the time.")

The fact that American culture has conflicting standards of polite behavior only reinforces my argument that appropriate behavior must sometimes be situational and subjective, not culturally determined.

EMERGENCY SITUATIONS

Most of the time, when you are angry you can go off someplace appropriate and discharge your emotion. But in an emergency when you have a strong surge of present-moment anger, you may find it appropriate or necessary to express the anger right away.

Consider the following examples:

What Do You Do If ... ?

- ... you drive crosstown to buy your friend a nice shirt and the prices are out of sight?

Keep breathing.

If that's not enough to get the anger from your body, say aloud, to no one in particular, "I'm so angry now. The prices are too high!"

This is appropriate behavior. You have stated your feelings without shaming any particular person. You have not said anything our culture considers offensive (as you would if you had said, "These prices are too [swear word] high!").

• . . . People are telling jokes you find offensive?

Keep breathing.

If that's not sufficient to get the anger from your body, say, "I'm offended by those jokes, guys. Knock it off."

• . . . people are making comments you consider racist or sexist?

Keep breathing.

If that's not sufficient to get the anger from your body, say, "I'm offended by your comments. I don't want to hear people disparaged because they are" women, Jews, blacks, handicapped, or whatever. "I need you to talk about something else."

• . . . you look out the window and see a father beating his seven-year-old child?

Keep breathing.

Feel what your body is telling you. Maybe you don't need to do anything because your sense of peace and well-being isn't threatened by a child being hit. I've seen children psychologically abused—screamed at and told they're bad—and not felt moved to do anything. I'm not proud of this, but it's the truth.

But I don't think I could see a child physically beaten. I think I'd feel that the child's welfare was as much my responsibility at that moment as his or her father's, because I had clarity of mind and the father had lost his to rage. If I thought the father might do serious physical damage to the child—if he were using a stick or a strop, say—I'd call the police before I did anything else.

Whether or not I called the police, I *think*—I'm not sure

because I'm glad to say it hasn't happened—I would then have to confront the man. I would do this in full awareness that I was doing something dangerous and something that went against my own rule of having as little as possible to do with unsafe people.

I'd say something like, "Stop it! I can't watch this happen. I need you to stop."

Being *seen* by someone else will often stop an abuser. He can feel your energy and know he is violating *your* boundaries. If he has any sense, he will see that he is also violating his *victim's* boundaries, and stop. Incidentally, it appears that a male abuser is more likely to stop when the outsider seeing his abuse is a woman. Women police officers are better than male officers at stopping family violence without being drawn into it.

If the abuser doesn't stop when you tell him to, you'll need to feel what's right for you to do. It may be nothing—you may walk away. You may stay and watch, a witness to the wrong. You may start crying or call out to the child to cry, not to hold his or her suffering in. You may say you're going to call the police or have already called them. You may decide you have to put *your* body on the line and risk bodily injury to stop bodily injury—injury to the child and to you, from your anger and pain at seeing the wrong and swallowing your emotions.

Before I'd put my body on the line, I'd tell the abuser what I was doing. I'd say something like, "I have to try and stop you. It's that disturbing to me. I don't want to hurt you. I just want you to stop." I like to think I'd be nonviolently physical, hold the man's arms, and not hit him. Not try to punish him— just keep him from punishing his child.

It's impossible to know what one will do in an emergency situation of this kind. But it's important to remember three things.

First, whatever you do should be in response to your deepest feelings, not sentimental notions of what you "ought" to feel. We ought to feel a lot of things we don't—about the world's forty thousand children under six who die every day of hunger, disease, and neglect, for example, or the tens of millions of Americans working full time who can't afford medical insurance for their families. The world is full of wrongs that cry out to be fixed, but you shouldn't start to fix them unless you feel you have to. Unless your feelings drive you to it, you aren't your brother's keeper or a beaten child's defender.

Second, your primary responsibility is to protect yourself—even against behavior prompted by your own emotions if this behavior would lead you into jeopardy. You are angry about what the father is doing, but the father is far beyond anger, in a hot or cold rage that demands that he inflict pain on others. Expressing your anger to him could get you maimed or killed. You may decide that the best thing for you to do is back off and stifle your anger.

Which leads to my last point. The feelings that you *can't* get out at the time of the emergency should be expressed as soon as possible thereafter, and as strongly as need be.

People who work at jobs with a great deal of stress—police officers; urban firefighters; emergency room, geriatric ward, and hospice workers; prison guards; flight controllers—need safe places to discharge their emotions after work. But then, maybe most of us need such places these days, so high-pressure have all our lives become. Far better to scream in a car, beat a pillow, twist a towel, chop wood, or do a frantic dance than do the typical after-work relaxer of ''unwinding'' with a drink, which does nothing but suppress emotions that need to be released.

14

Managing Anger
at Work

You miss your bus. The photocopier breaks down. A co-worker you respect is fired. Another fails to come through on an assignment she absolutely *promised*. The coffee in your office tastes like sweaty socks, and the Danishes are stale. Good old Bubba claims to have a hernia, so you have to do all the lifting. Your assistant steals your idea, reports it to the boss, and gets the assignment you wanted.

Life at work is no less unfair and annoying—infuriating!—than the rest of life. And we spend half our waking hours there.

What can we do about it?

The usual:

1. *Realize* what we feel rather than deny it. Admit it and embrace it.
2. *Feel* it, and express our feelings in safe and responsible ways.

Say you're a waiter, and you're serving a party of six impossible people. When your body tells you the stress of their demanding selfishness is getting to you, pay attention; acknowledge what you feel. Slip into the men's room, put a rolled-up napkin in your mouth, flush the toilet, and scream, biting down. Scream and bite till your gut and jaw can't do any more at that time. Two minutes of that, and you'll go back to work feeling ten times better than if you hadn't done it. Incidentally, if you open your mouth, tense your face, push air up from your diaphragm, and scream without using your vocal cords, so that the only sound you produce is a sharp *"Ehhhh!"* of escaping air, you will have done your body nearly as much good as you would screaming aloud.

Say you're a woman lawyer, and a male judge is calling you "honey" and "sweetheart." You find this offensive and say something like, "Your Honor, I prefer to be referred to as 'Counselor' or 'Ms. Davis' not by a term of endearment." But the judge is a none-too-bright white-haired oldster to whom you can't teach new tricks; he continues to call you "honey" and "dear." You finally decide that if you make any more protests, you may jeopardize your client's case. What to do?

If your anger is such that you can't contain it, request an emergency recess, hurry to your car parked in the basement, get into the back seat, close the door, and pound the cushion as hard and fast as you can. Yell, if that helps.

Whatever your job, you can find a way to get free for a couple of minutes and release your anger in a responsible way. Often, of course, you will feel strong enough to hold in your emotion till the end of the work day, then get rid of it by doing anger-release exercises at home, in the gym, or on the hike-and-bike trail.

If you're a housewife or househusband, you have privacy and flexibility of schedule; you of all workers ought to be able to get rid of your frustrations and rage without involving other people. If you are a parent, it is crucial that you do this, because if you don't discharge your negative emotions yourself, you are likely to inflict them on your children as slaps, cruel words, hostile inattention.

When I speak of anger release in the work context, I am speaking of something we've all heard about: stress management. Stress is the great incubator of present anger, and, as we've seen, if present anger isn't discharged right away or soon after it arises, it gets buried, festers, and comes out in an inappropriate way somewhere down the line.

So everything that reduces stress—like getting enough exercise and rest, and enough intellectual, spiritual, and sexual stimulation—reduces your susceptibility to present anger. Further, discharging past anger brings down your stress level, making you less vulnerable to present annoyances.

One stress-reducer I haven't said much about is eating a healthy diet. Sugar constricts the blood vessels in the body—so does caffeine. Anything that constricts the blood going to your brain and heart reduces your ability to handle stress. Healthy foods, on the other hand, relax your system. Eating a banana, which is rich in potassium, before you go to bed is like drinking warm milk: It will help you sleep.

Nicotine also constricts your blood vessels. Smokers say cigarettes help them relax, but what actually happens is that the nicotine numbs them down so they don't feel how tense they actually are.

Eat healthy meals—and healthy snacks too. Vegetables like carrots and celery and cauliflower and broccoli are much better for you than candy, coffee, and chocolate cake; they also make a satisfying noise when you bite them. If you need more energy, eat a piece of fruit or some raisins or pretzels or nuts.

I can't mention healthy foods without adding that some of those foods, like milk and grains and nuts, are viciously *unhealthy* for some people. Food allergies are much more widespread than conventional medicine believes. I have a friend who is allergic to almonds and who has almost died on two occasions because restaurants used almond paste in their cooking and assured him they hadn't. The friends who have helped me most with this book, Dan Jones and Bill Stott, are both allergic to wheat and get depressed if they eat it. The best estimate is that 50 percent of Americans are wheat allergic (wheat is a grass, after all, like hay and ragweed, to which so many of us are allergic) though few people have cerebral allergies as Dan and Bill do. If you're eating healthy foods and still feel lousy, consider seeing an allergist, nutritionist, or holistic medical practitioner.

HIGH-STRESS JOBS

Reducing stress is important for all jobs, but it can be a matter of life and death in jobs like medical and police work.

Consider what happens to the intensive-care nurse or social worker or hospice volunteer or minister or pediatrician when a client dies. Consider the EMS paramedic who brings in carloads of New Year's Eve accident victims. Consider probation officers, prison guards, police and firefighters who risk their lives every day and sometimes get laughed at or taunted for doing so. Because of their work, all these people are compelled to take in huge amounts of tension, sadness, anger, hatred, disgust, and they must find ways to release these emotions or they risk cracking up mentally and physically. The doctors most likely to commit suicide are, significantly, psychiatrists, who listen to their patients' emotions and try to show the patients by their non-reaction that the "rational" way to deal with emotions is to hold them in.

No, the rational way to deal with emotions is to feel and express them, and because it is, people in high stress jobs must take special care *not* to spend all their time in their heads. Many police departments and some hospitals provide a gym where the staff can work out and thus get tension out of their bodies. That is good, but not enough. I look forward to the day when police departments and hospitals and hospices and prisons will have an emotional release room in which staff members are encouraged to cry and rage and shout and twist towels and punch a pillow or a punching bag as their bodies feel the need to.

HOW OFTEN DO YOU NEED TO RELEASE YOUR ANGER?

The simple answer here is, as often as you need to. It depends on you and your job. If your work is very high stress, you may need to discharge your feelings every day, even twice a day. If you have a calm temperament and a job without much stress, you may be able to go for a month or more.

Again, if you pay attention to your body, it will tell you when you need to cry or scream or pound something.

Harvey Jackins and his reevaluation counseling recommend that people have an emotional discharge every week to get rid of the unhealthy emotions they are holding in. This seems like good general advice to me. I know I feel best and work best when I either cry or yell or beat a pillow every five to seven days. When I'm at my worst, it's because I haven't taken the time to do emotional release for three or four weeks.

This chapter's message is simple: Just because you're at work doesn't mean you're not living real life. The emotions brought up at work need to be processed just like the emotions brought up everywhere else.

15
Managing Anger
in Love

Anger in love? But of course. Anger begins in love—begins because the loved one, generally the infant's mother, denies the infant what he or she desires. The infant rages because the world isn't made to its wishes, Momma isn't always there and doesn't do exactly what the infant thinks she should.

Nearly all love relationships start with a repeat of our infant link to Mama. We fall in love partly because we hope to repair something that didn't work in childhood. To some degree, we are looking for the Mama we didn't have to give us the unconditional love we didn't get then. Needless to say, the Mama we fall in love with as adults can be male or female, depending on our sexual orientation. The problem is, this Mama doesn't exist. Darned few adults can give unconditional love to their children, much less other adults.

Ernest Hemingway's third wife, Martha Gellhorn, divorced him, she said, because she found she couldn't worship him twenty-four hours a day—twelve hours, yes, but not twenty-four—and twenty-four was what he wanted.

It's what *everybody* wants: *Total* love from another person.

In the first blush of love, in the "romance" period, we think maybe this time we're going to get it. The beloved so entirely accepts us, *magnifies* us, that we give ourselves over to him or her. Whatever the beloved does seems miraculously what we want.

During this phase we see in the beloved all the good things we want and can't provide for ourselves. As the psychologists say, we "project" ourselves onto the beloved. For example, I, a careful and orderly person, look at a woman I love and see in her the reckless spontaneity I've never allowed myself. I am wildly attracted. Six months later, when the projection has worn off and the romantic phase is over, I look at her, and what had seemed enchantingly spontaneous now looks chaotic, irresponsible, dangerous. What I had loved about her has become something I always fear: unreliability.

Why does the romantic phase end? Ah, that is the question poets and song writers have been asking since Homer: "Where has my true love gone?" "Who knows how to make love stay?" "Where is the *love*?"

Romance ends—Freud would argue—because the pressure of reality is too strong for it to last. Psychologists say that the period of romantic projection can last for three to six months. A cynical female client I once worked with said it lasted eleven weeks—after that, she made her lovers move out because, she said, she knew "the good times were over and the shit would start."

In fact, the romance phase can last longer, even years, if the couple lives apart and only sees each other from time to time. With daily contact, though, a romantic projection breaks down pretty quickly. "No man is a hero to his valet," says the old song. No lover is miraculous when he or she shares your bathroom.

The romance phase is followed by anger and grief and, often, the end of the relationship. "How could a love that seemed so right go wrong?" a 1950s song asks. When the romantic projection fails, when we see that this other person is not and is never going to be the parent we always wanted, we feel as Adam and Eve felt when they were kicked out of the Garden. Our infantile rage says: "What happened? We should still be in paradise. Paradise should always continue.'' ''Where is the life that late I led?'' (Cole Porter) ''I can't get no satisfaction.'' (Mick Jagger)

Anger and grief are appropriate responses to being kicked out of Eden, and if we don't *feel* this anger and grief and work through them, we will give in to bitterness and cynicism—like the woman did who said love lasted eleven weeks, period—or, to say the same thing, we will die.

What finally overwhelms our romantic projection is the fact of our beloved's *otherness*. We finally start to see our lover as a person apart from us and our needs. We see that he or she is flawed, is human, did not come into this world to meet our needs all day long. Our parents were supposed to do that when we were infants and toddlers, and if they had done so, our need for our lover to do it now would be far less than it is. If we understand this, it would greatly reduce our anger and grief when the beloved lets us down. We'd say, ''Aw, my lover is just a person—flawed and human like all of us. I understand that.''

TO LET YOUR LOVER BE HIMSELF OR HERSELF . . .

. . . takes enormous maturity. Because every part of you cries out to have your lover be as he or she *seemed to be* at the start of your courtship, when you projected what you wanted or, too often, *needed* onto him or her.

Until we are mature—that is, fully accepting of ourselves—our love relations are a battle for control. You want your lovers to be as you want, and vice versa. You try to push them into the roles you want, and they won't be pushed. Instead, they get angry that you won't see and accept them as they are. They feel themselves back in the tight black box of their birth family, where they were compelled to be a good little false self for their parents so as to meet their parents' needs.

You are angry because your lover isn't any longer what you thought he or she was. Your lover is angry at you for the same reason. And now, just when your relationship is getting real, it may collapse, because one or both of you, disappointed in your expectations and angry at the other's expectations, start thinking and perhaps talking about ending the relationship. One of you may say, "If things don't get better, I'm out of here." What you mean is, "If you don't do more of what I want, I'm leaving." The possibility of abandonment is in the air, and with it comes more anger.

A large percentage of relationships shipwreck at this point. Lovers start looking for *new* lovers to meet their impossible dreams. Or the relationship declines into make-believe: "I'll pretend that you are as I want you to be and I am happy, if you'll pretend that I am as you want me to be and *you* are happy." In still other relationships, the couple seeks outside help from a counselor or therapist to renegotiate the ground rules so that both partners may get a little more of what each wants.

I believe in outside help to clarify both lovers' wants and see if there is a way they can be partially met. More important, though, I think, is for each partner in the relationship to see that the problem is *his* or *her* own.

Each partner has to say to himself or herself something like, "I'm angry because my lover tries to control me all the time [or won't do what I want]. But before I try to change her [or him], I've got to deal with my feelings of anger and resentment and betrayal. I've got to get these feelings out because until I do, I will be a victim of them. I'll be angry because of his [or her] control, manipulation, irresponsibility, threats of abandonment. I'll be my lover's victim, my emotions controlled by what she [or he] does.

"Only when I've admitted what I feel, embraced it, and gotten it out of my system can I take charge of my life and begin to understand how I got involved with someone like him [or her] who's such a control freak [or lone wolf]."

When you have felt your feelings deeply enough and expressed them from your body—and thus *possessed* them instead of being possessed *by* them—you may be able to tell your lover about them. Do this. But don't expect your lover to change; he or she probably won't. (This will only produce more anger in you that you'll have to deal with.)

What your lover will do if he or she has any sensitivity at all is to see that *you've* changed. You no longer wait for him or her to meet your unfulfilled childhood needs. You are like an Al-Anon member who has dealt so deeply with herself that her husband's alcohol intake no longer affects her. No matter how your lover behaves—controlling, cold-shouldering, abandoning—you will be okay. "I see that you're trying to manipulate me," you may say when you catch your lover at it. "That no longer bothers me. I'm going to do what I feel is right for me. I don't need your approval, and your disapproval no longer hurts because I've discharged so much of the pain and anger that I felt growing up always being the bad child in the family."

AFTER ROMANCE

After romance, love is work. Love is a commitment to someone else for better or worse, richer or poorer, healthy or sick. (Have you seen the recitation of the marriage vows make grown men and women—married *and* single—cry? I have.)

Real love is tough, because it's a making-do with less than you wanted. You wanted your husband to be interested only in you, and here he is flirting with the waitress. What are you going to do with your anger—throw water in his face and get up and leave? Or are you going to see that your anger has more to do with you and your childhood need to be paid attention to than with your spouse, who is engaging in teasing behavior natural to humans and other advanced animals? Are you going to rid yourself of your anger and pain, or are you going to insist that your husband try to do it—say, by begging for your forgiveness and promising never to have eye contact with another woman?

Real love knows that its romantic need of the other is unhealthy and counterproductive. If your lover *were* able to be what you want and to present you with just the emotional feedback you seek, you would come to resent, even hate him or her. Why? Because he or she would be doing work you should be doing—doing your feeling for you!—and thus infantilizing you. Likewise, if one member of a couple does all the *thinking* for the other—takes charge of work, finances, and the children's education—the other member will be angry because he or she isn't getting to be an adult.

And the longer a relationship lasts, the more anger, even hatred, there is likely to be within a couple. If you've been with the same partner for twenty or thirty years, you're going to have a history of negative feelings toward him or her that is nearly as heavy as your history with your parents. And if your parents didn't set you a healthy example, you won't know that negative feelings are okay and that normal people feel love and hate for everybody who's important to them. The ability to hold such paradoxical emotions is, as psychologist Robert Johnson puts it, "the measure of our spiritual strength and the surest sign of maturity."

Nonetheless, having acknowledged and felt your negative emotions toward your lover, you have to get rid of them—twist and shout them out of your body—or they will fester and perhaps explode. If you don't discharge past anger, then you'll mix your anger at your mate for something he does in 1993 with the anger you have about something he did in 1982 or 1971 or both. You're liable to vent a rage disproportionate to its present cause, and in an inappropriate way. You will embitter your relationship with old, hidden grievances instead of keeping it healthy and intimate by revealing your *present* feelings, including anger, to the person with whom you are making your life.

Am I saying that you should never end a love relationship? No. People grow and change in different ways and different rates. You may find that you and your beloved have moved so far apart that the only honest thing to do is separate.

What I am saying is that if you leave a love relationship because of problems that you blame or hold the other person responsible for, you will find those problems repeated in your *next* relationship and all subsequent ones until you realize the problem is in you and that only you can deal with it.

THE ONLY HEALTHY WAY TO *START* A LOVE RELATIONSHIP...

. . . is to be over your former relationships. This takes time and work and pain. And most people are too impatient and needy to wait: They plunge into a new romance before they are ready to love again— before they are even ready to date!

When are you ready to date? My answer is pretty radical: You're ready to date when you don't *have* to date. When you're happy dancing in the kitchen by yourself, you're ready to dance with someone else.

Most people don't give themselves nearly enough *personal* time between relationships. To be really ready to love again, you have to:

- Be rid of your debilitating addictions: to alcohol, drugs, food, and sexual excess.
- Exercise more than you have been.
- Eat a healthy diet.
- Establish a spiritual connection to something larger than you— which doesn't have to be God, which could be life, nature, the environment, the poor, human suffering, or important dead relatives and friends in your past.

and then you must:

- Grieve out the sadness of your last love relationship and any earlier relationship that clings in your memory.
- Discharge the anger you have concerning those relationships.
- Forgive yourself for the "mistakes" you made in those relationships so thoroughly that you come to realize you didn't make *any* mistakes: that, given who you were then and what

you knew then, you could not have done any better than you
did.
- Forgive your former lover. Now, please understand that this
  doesn't mean you have to actually *see* or talk to your former
  lover. It is often healthier to communicate with him or her by
  letter or just in your mind. Tell him or her your gratitude for
  the time and love you shared. Say—and mean it!—''I thank
  you. I love you. I forgive you. I wish you everything you
  want. I let you go.''

It's a tough assignment. Doing it takes time and large quantities
of emotional release. Getting over a past love relationship can be
enormously helped by psychotherapy and emotional-release work,
twelve-step meetings, singles support counseling, and divorce recovery groups. Based on my own experience and that of friends and
clients, I believe that an ended relationship can be emotionally cleared
out in as little as two or three months, *if*—and it's a huge *if*—your
present loss isn't tied to:

- infant abandonment (because you had the typical pre-1970s
  unempathetic mother)
- childhood deprivation (for example, the death of a parent or
  your parents' divorce)
- a bad experience (a nasty jilting, say) in your first love

IF YOUR PRESENT LOSS IS TIED TO A PAST LOSS THAT YOU HAVEN'T WORKED THROUGH...

...it will almost certainly take you much longer to get over the
present loss.

Consider Betty, who was dropped by her boyfriend, Jeff, a year
ago. Today she's still furious at him, weeping much of the day,
gorging on chocolate (for the sugar and caffeine high), and nearly
always depressed, sometimes suicidal. Her friends wonder why she

can't get her life together. They recommend that she do the healthy sorts of things I've listed above, and Betty tries—but nothing helps her much.

I suspect that Betty is using Jeff's abandonment to deal with another, earlier loss (or losses). Perhaps her mother nursed her on a strict schedule, no matter how much Betty cried. Perhaps her father left her family, died, or soldiered in Vietnam for a year when she was six. Perhaps her first boyfriend pulled out much the same way Jeff did.

Because Betty didn't deal sufficiently with her early losses, didn't grieve and rage and thus discharge them, she has done what psychologists from Freud to Harville Hendrix say we all do with our traumatic suffering: She has unconsciously arranged her life with Jeff in such a way that she will get a chance to suffer again and *recapitulate* her abandonment, so that maybe this time she will handle it better.

Betty has lots of work to do to be able to stand on her own two feet, a happy, self-actualizing person. She is dangerously likely to fall in love with the first man who smiles at her, and she is a danger to any man attracted to her, because she will cling so hard and need so much attention that in all likelihood he will find he has to leave her, as Jeff did, to keep his soul his own.

THE ESSENTIALS OF A HEALTHY LOVE RELATIONSHIP

I am going to give five rules for a good love relationship.

1. See your lover as himself or herself. DON'T READ INTO HIS OR HER BEHAVIOR WHAT OTHER PEOPLE HAVE DONE OR NOT DONE. Anytime you see your partner as someone other than he or she is—as, say, your mother or father, or an earlier lover—the result, for both you and your lover, will be anger or sadness or both.

2. Don't expect your lover to heal you of your wounds. That is your business. Expect no more than that your lover will be sympathetic and supportive of you as you do the work you need to do to heal.

3. Be sympathetic and supportive to your lover, but don't try to change him or her. Any attempt to do this will cause him or her to be angry and will also show that you are still caught up in a past relationship, probably to one or both of your parents.

Say to your lover early in your relationship and often thereafter things like, "Honey, I love you and I want you to know me. I'm going to tell you [or *I am telling you*] my feelings, my past, my relationships, and exactly what I'm feeling now. But I won't tell you *your* feelings or judge you or your past, and I don't expect you to tell me my feelings or judge me."

If you break this rule and criticize your lover, you'll create anger and hostility, because everybody wants to be responsible for his or her own version of reality and truth. When someone tries to tell you what you're feeling, you're shoved back into childhood, where other people (your parents) determined your "truth." And this has got to bring up infantile rage because you're not being seen as *you*.

4. If you must speak critically to your lover, speak about things that just happened. As: "Dammit, Stanley, I'm angry. You promised to clean up after your poker party and you didn't." DON'T MAKE A LAUNDRY LIST OF OLD GRIEVANCES ("It's like when you promised to get Bobby a football and forgot") OR GLOBALIZE ("You always say you'll do something and you never do") OR SHAME ("Can't you think of *anybody* else but you?") OR JUDGE OR NAME-CALL ("You're just a slob—world class!").

Feelings are simple: anger, joy, boredom, excitement. The more words you use to express painful feelings, the more likely it is you're importing *old* buried stuff. When your feelings aren't happy, talking about them *less* is more.

Further, *explaining* why you feel you must criticize another person is always more about trying to change his or her behavior than about getting your feelings out. Indeed, a huge proportion of criticism happens because the people doing the criticizing are trying to *avoid* dealing with what they're feeling.

5. To see whether you're in command of your anger—which is to say, whether your anger is present-tense anger—see if you are able to postpone discussing it. For example, if you can say, "Mark, I'm very angry and I want to talk to you about it when we get home,'' you are in a much healthier place than if you have to say, ''Mark, I'm very angry and we've got to deal with this right now. If you walk out the door without our having resolved it, don't bother to come back.'' Anyone that angry either has his or her life in jeopardy or is suffering from more than a present injury.

TO REPEAT: LOVE IS TOUGH

No reason to pretend otherwise. The beatniks, who were otherwise not known for their sensitivity to human limitations, referred to love as ''work.''

To make the love commitment is to say ''I accept you just as you are, however you are. I accept whatever you do so long as I don't feel hurt by it. And even if I do feel hurt by it, even if I disapprove of what you do, even if I choose not to stay with you, I accept you. To me, the most important thing about you is that you be able to be who you are, and the most important thing to me is that I get to be who I am. And anything less than this will always produce anger between us.''

16
Firing Someone and Ending a Relationship

This chapter is 10 percent philosophy, 90 percent how-to. It tells you how you can protect yourself and other people in two situations where anger is *always* close to the surface:

1. When you're firing somebody.
2. When you want to make a change in a romantic relationship.

Let's begin with the philosophy.

ASSUMPTIONS

You are trying to get out of either an economic or a romantic relationship. You want to get out as smoothly as possible—that is, with as little pain as possible for you and the other person. You can't avoid causing pain, but to keep pain to a minimum, you must try not to attack the other person. In fact, you should try to talk about the other person as little as possible.

Instead:

- If your relationship to the other person is economic, talk about the job.
- If your relationship to the other person is romantic, talk about yourself and your feelings.

This sounds odd, but it works.

FIRING SOMEONE

The most helpful book I know on how to fire people is *Mayor,* Edward Koch's story of his years as mayor of New York City. Koch says, "There are very few people in government who are capable of firing." Actually, there are few people capable of this anywhere. He describes ugly, angry, counterproductive firings done by other politicians.

One chapter in Koch's book, called "Reorganizing the Administration," describes how he fired most of his chief assistants and reassigned the others. Making such changes is *tough,* he says. It's like having a cyst that you know has to be lanced: "worry, worry, worry, painful, painful, painful, piercing. And then all the pus runs out and you feel better." So skillful was Koch at this particular reorganization that nearly everyone he fired cooperated in the change, and he stayed friends with most of them.

Koch doesn't give a script of the things a boss should say when firing someone, but in his own firings he seems to have made all the following statements as many times as was necessary until the fired person realized there was no point in arguing further:

- "Things aren't working out, and I am going to make some changes, including you."
- "Nothing you can say will change my mind."

- "This has nothing to do with you personally. We just don't see the job the same way."
- "When something doesn't work we have to end it, but I hope we can do it the best possible way for you, because I don't want to hurt you unnecessarily."
- "I've told you how I want the job done, and you want to do it your way. I respect your not being willing to do it my way, and I know that if you tried to, you wouldn't do it well because your heart wouldn't be in it."

Note that although the conflict between boss and worker may be over matters as concrete as the worker's lateness or sloppy work, a boss following Koch's strategy would speak as though the conflict were *ideological,* a difference of opinion. To a worker who is chronically late, a boss might say something like, "You and I disagree about when this office opens. I have told you nine o'clock many times. You usually arrive about ten. I've given you three warnings, and now I've decided to make a change." To a worker doing sloppy work, a boss might say, "I've showed you the kind of work we require. You have a different standard, which is no doubt fine at some other company. But it's not fine here, and I have decided to let you go. Nothing personal—we just don't agree on what's acceptable."

The following excerpt describes Koch's firing of Robert Milano, his deputy mayor for economic development. You will note the five themes mentioned above playing through the conversation and see how emotionally rough even a competent firing can be:

I called [Milano] in. He had no idea what the appointment was about. I was told he also wanted to see me about his plans to add people to [the Economic Development office]. He was rather exuberant as he walked in the door. Before he sat down, I said, "Bob, it is not working and we have to end it. Let's figure out the best way for you." You could almost hear the pain that had struck him when he realized he was being fired. That is what I mean by saying it isn't easy.

He said, "I can't believe it. What's wrong?"

"Bob," I said, "we don't agree. I believe [the Economic Development office] should be twelve people who are lean and hungry. You believe there should be two hundred or four hundred people. That is a bureaucracy, and I don't want it. I have been telling and telling you that. And you continue to take a tack that is not what I want."

"Well, can't we change it?" he said. "Can't we do what you want?"

I said, "No. If something doesn't work, you have to end it. It won't do any good now to decide you are going to do what I want. Because you won't. It doesn't work that way. We don't look at things the same way, so let's end it. And let's end it in a nice way so that you are not embarrassed."

And then he broke into tears. I was very much distressed. It is very hard for me to see an adult cry. Then he said, "You have disgratadadoed me!"

I said to myself, I've what? Apparently what he was saying was I had disgraced him in Italian. I asked myself, Jesus Christ, what am I in for?

But that was a passing moment. He composed himself and said he was sorry he had broken down, that it had never happened to him before. Then he said, "Fine. I understand now, and I agree. I will leave."

But it rarely works out that way. He left and then he held a press conference denouncing me and saying that I knew nothing about economic development and how he knew everything and how I was standing in the way. It was just foolish. And of course, the reporters came running over to me, as they always will in such a case, and asked that I respond to his denunciation.

My response was "I will not add to his agony."

Koch understands that a boss has the right to judge a subordinate's performance—foolish, magnificent, slovenly—but not the subordinate's *person.* Employees may be fired but not humiliated.

ENDING A ROMANTIC RELATIONSHIP

Ending a romantic relationship is much more difficult than ending an economic one because our *persons,* our private selves, are inevitably involved. When Jill leaves John, it's hard for John to see her action as other than a judgment on him—unless Jill is clever and strenuously (and correctly) blames *herself.*

This is what you should do when you want to break off a romantic relationship. Don't blame the other person. Stay focused on yourself. Which is to say, tell the truth about what is driving you to want to break up.

But don't say, "Honey, I don't find you attractive anymore." Don't say, "I'm tired of our life together—it's *boring.*"

Saying these things makes it sound as though the other person's at fault for your wanting to end the relationship. And they are not— you're the one who wants out. *You* and your feelings are the problem. So talk about those feelings.

Don't talk about feelings in the past, however. Don't say, "Our relationship was doomed from the start because . . . " Those past feelings didn't drive you to break off the relationship then. You may not have even *spoken* of those feelings then. The only feelings that count are the ones at work now—the ones pushing you to end the relationship.

So if you are willing to take the time to try and end the relationship gently, I would recommend you say something like:

"Honey, you know how much I care for you. But I'm finding there are ways our relationship has gone dead for me. I may not always feel this, but I want you to know what I'm feeling now. I'm feeling that I'm going to want to change our relationship. I want you to know that I realize this isn't your fault. You're not in any way to blame. It isn't *my* fault, either, really. I don't want to be feeling it.

"It's something in me I have to deal with. I'm sorry about it, and I'm having lots of feelings about it that make me sad and angry and ashamed. I know I need to do something about these feelings, and I'm starting to do it.

"I want you to know I'm dealing with these things and that I'm going to tell you what I find out. I don't know what's going to come out of my feelings, obviously, because I haven't gotten there yet. I don't know whether I'm going to be feeling this next week or next month. I might, I might not. But I wanted to be open with you and tell you what I'm feeling now."

At this point the other person may explode in anger or tears. In which case, *protect yourself*. You are dealing with a person who is, at least temporarily, unsafe.

Say, "Now, wait a minute. I'm not blaming you for what I feel. I'm saying you're *not* responsible. I'm telling you what *I'm* feeling. I have a total right to my feelings. You have a total right to your feelings. If you tell me your feelings in an appropriate way, not trying to hurt me, I'll be glad to hear them."

If the person rages or wailingly accuses you, leave. As you do so, do *not* say over your shoulder, "We'll talk about this when you've gotten hold of yourself." That's an attack. Say, "We'll talk about this when I feel safe enough to hear you."

If the other person doesn't explode in anger or tears, he or she may be strong enough to be emotionally safe on this issue. If so, you can have a civilized conversation.

The other person is of course greatly disturbed to hear about your feelings and may say, "Do you want a divorce?" Or, "Are you going to move out?"

To which I recommend you respond, "I don't know. I'm not clear about my feelings yet."

In all likelihood, this is the truth. Very few of us know what we're going to be feeling the day after tomorrow, to say nothing of next month. Saying "I don't know" is expressing honestly what you're feeling at the moment.

The other person may then want to know if the problem is money, sex, routine, some combination thereof, or something else.

To which, if you judge the other person safe enough, you may respond by telling more truth. As, for example:

"No, I don't feel too bad about the money. It's true that we don't agree about what to spend it on or how we want to live. But I don't think those things are what's crucial to me.''

Or, ''Well, yeah, I'm really concerned about my lack of interest in sex. We've had wonderful fun in bed, and I don't know why that's gone from me now.''

Or, ''Yes, I am attracted to you. Not as much as before, though, and I want to check out my feelings about this.''

Or, ''Bored? I guess so. I think *restless* is a better word for it. You know I keep thinking that in fifty years I'll be under the ground, and I won't have done enough with the life I have now. I just want more, and I feel maybe I've got to go look for it.''

Or even, ''Yes, there is someone else. I don't know how much this other person means to me. This is something I have to work out.''

After you've told the truth this way, whatever feelings the other person has are his or her responsibility, because you haven't said that the other person is the problem.

You have said, ''This is what I'm feeling now. The problem is mine. I'm doing something about it, and I'll resolve it. You can't do anything to help me, except allow me to keep telling you what I'm feeling.''

Over the next days, weeks, even months, you will of course work to learn what your feelings really are. You may make progress reports to the other person if he or she can hear them without punishing you.

When you're finally clear on what you feel and what you want to do about your feelings, tell the other person. If you choose to break off the relationship, you say something like, ''You know what I've been going through because I've told you about my feelings. Well, now I've decided it's time for me to move on. I'm clear I no longer want to be in the relationship we've had. This isn't because of you. It's not your fault. I take full responsibility for the decision. There's nothing you can do about it, nothing you can 'fix,' nothing you can change or become. This is me.''

Then talk about your gratitude for the relationship you've had with the other person and the terms on which you hope the relationship will continue, if you want it to.

In this context, it may or may not be a solace to you or the other person to know that psychologists believe that every relationship we remember hasn't ended for us. Though we are separated from the other person, even by death, the relationship continues to evolve in us as long as we bring it to mind. Divorce, for most people, is just a different kind of marriage.

17
Anger and Your Children

You already know how crucial I consider the parent-child relationship, so you won't be surprised that I wanted this chapter in the book. You may be surprised that the chapter comes so *late* in the book, after I've given my views about appropriate and inappropriate ways of being angry with other people.

The reason is simple: Your children aren't "other people." Parent-child relationships are special. Adults can choose whom they relate to—and don't relate to—when they decide this is in their best interest. Children cannot make these choices: They do not choose their parents and must try to grow into emotional self-sufficiency (which many people never do) before they are free from the need to relate to or rebel against their parents.

Further, adults can avoid criticizing other people and their behavior (though in fact few people do). Parents can avoid criticizing their children—and should—but are expected to comment on their children's behavior—and should—because they, as parents, are responsible for teaching their children what is acceptable and appropriate, and what isn't.

Thanks to our culture's misguided values and poisonous parenting methods, being a child is misery for most children much of the time. Though we adults like to pretend this isn't true, most of us know in our hearts that it is. We remember. We can never forget.

Being a child is hard, and being a parent is no picnic either. I know a man who fought in the infantry in World War II, killed enemy soldiers in close combat, saw his buddies killed and badly wounded, and went five months without a bath. He says nothing in his life has been as difficult as having a 14-year-old son.

This chapter discusses how to be angry with your child, how to help your child be angry, and how to make amends to your child for mistakes you have made, whether from anger or some other cause.

IF YOU ARE ANGRY WITH YOUR CHILD...

First, be careful. Being inappropriately angry with someone else may hurt him or her. Being inappropriately angry with your child, especially while the child is young, can devastate him or her. It can ruin his or her life. Estimates are that more than 60 percent of all depressives, 80 percent of all prisoners, and 90 percent of all suicides had parents who were inappropriately angry or inappropriately intimate with them.

If you are angry with your child, take big breaths, in and out. *Feel* what you're feeling, and if it's so strong that it will hurt your child, get away fast and express the feeling in a safe way, by yourself.

Second, do as psychologist Haim Ginott said: Be angry at what your child has done, but never at the child himself or herself.

If your four-year-old daughter throws food on the floor, don't curse a blue streak and scream, "Bad girl!" But don't coo, "What a little piglet!" either, because this would mislead your daughter into thinking you *liked* what she did, thought it was a cute way to gain attention. Ginott would say that a parent shouldn't criticize *or* praise a child— only what the child has done. The child's self should always be loved and accepted and never be up for discussion.

Say something like, "Food isn't for throwing, Vanessa. You know that. We throw balls, not food. Come help me clean it up."

If your seventeen-year-old son leaves the car a mess, don't curse a blue streak and scream "You pig!" Instead, say something like, "There's a lot of your stuff in the car, Jason. I'm using the car in an hour, and I count on you to have it picked up by then."

Third, remember your priorities. A clean car counts, but a lot less than Jason. It would be nice if Vanessa didn't toss food on the floor, but her being secure about your love and her right to be a child and childish without suffering terrible retribution is much more important.

An eight-year-old is playing horsey in the living room and accidentally knocks a vase off a table. The vase breaks. In many American homes, that child is punished—shamed, spanked, sent to bed without dinner. What does the punishment show the child?

"I can be punished for anything, even if I didn't mean to do it."

What else does it show?

"The vase is worth more than I am."

This was one of the reasons I stopped going to the church I'd been going to: mistaken priorities. One day, a five-year-old started whimpering in the middle of the sermon. A few seconds after she started, her mother yanked her from the pew and out of the room. The minister had stopped talking, and we could hear the slap of the mother's hand on the child's flesh. The child started wailing.

The minister didn't pretend that nothing had happened. He interrupted the sermon and said the mother was to be commended for chastising her daughter, because children have to learn respect for their parents and for religion. Spare the rod and spoil the child.

Now, this was nearly twenty years ago. I didn't know then to ask myself, "Gosh, how about the girl? How is she going to feel about her mother's hurting her?" But I knew that if a minister condoned punishing innocent children, he wasn't somebody I wanted to listen to.

Parents think they have their children's best interests at heart, and they may have. But children have their own interests and priorities, and they have as much right to them as to their own feelings. This doesn't mean that children can *do* whatever they want. But when you find yourself in conflict with your child, ask yourself whether what the child wants to do jeopardizes his or her health and safety or violates your legitimate rights. If your answer to both questions is no, I suggest you let the child do it.

If you refuse to let your child do something simply because you prefer that he or she not do it, you may need to do some work on *your* feelings. What happened to you in the past that control, propriety, thrift, or neatness means so much? Who modeled such rigid behavior for you? Who gave you such high hurdles to jump?

As you grow older and understand better why you feel as you do, you may find that your priorities change, become more generous. A friend of mine began a second family at age forty-eight. He now has two sons under four. How differently he behaves toward them from the way he behaved toward his daughter and son of a generation ago!

"When Sarah and Brian were tots, they'd draw on the wall, as kids do, you know?" he tells me. "And I'd scream, 'Stop that! You're making a mess, damn it! That won't come off!' Now when my sons draw on the wall—a much more expensive wall, I must say, with antique wallpaper instead of paint—I say, 'Hmmmm. You know, that's *beautiful*. I mean, those shapes and colors. If I get you guys some Magic Markers, you think you'd do some more?'"

Now, please understand, I'm not saying that you should accept your child's *un*innocent misbehavior. If your child is malicious, if he or she is of the age to know better and intentionally smashes a vase or throws a baseball bat through a window, you do need to do something. First off, you need to find out what is troubling your child and try to help him or her cope with it.

Fourth, don't *punish*—discipline. Which means, set boundaries.

The difference between punishment and discipline is that punishment happens after the fact, for reasons that weren't made clear ahead of time. It is arbitrary and sometimes grossly excessive, and it belittles the child by depriving him or her of the means of controlling the world. Discipline, on the other hand, happens ahead of time, is explicit, and encourages growth by establishing meaningful choices.

Punishment says to a twelve-year-old, "Your room's a perfect mess. What am I going to do with you? You *never* do what I want. No camp for you this summer! That's all you understand."

Discipline tells a teenager, "If the car isn't cleaned up by two o'clock, you won't be able to use it this weekend."

Discipline establishes line-in-the-sand boundaries and gives the child the choice of respecting them or taking the consequences. If the child elects to take the consequences, that is his or her right. The parent should exact the consequences matter-of-factly, without browbeating or shaming the child.

It is right and proper for parents to discipline children in this way: to make clear what appropriate and inappropriate behavior is and what the consequences of both kinds of behavior are. As they grow older, children must of course have the right to discuss with their parents—and thus participate in—the setting of boundaries. At sixteen and seventeen, children should be setting most of their own boundaries. The best way for children to become self-governing adults is for them to start governing themselves as children.

Speaking of inappropriate things, that "punishment" speech given to the twelve-year-old with the messy room is a good example of what *not* to say to a child or anyone else. It is shaming—"What am I going to do with you?"—and full of exaggeration—"You *never* do what I want." And the punishment—"No camp for you this summer"—is so wildly out of proportion to the crime that it clearly will be rescinded.

Further, a strong argument can be made that children ten and older should be free to keep their rooms as they please, since they, not the parents, live there. My own feeling is that a parent who wants a child's room straightened up should say something like, "Paula, you know I want you to keep your room the way you want to. But when it gets into its current condition, I begin feeling the house is too small for me—you know, it's closing in! I wonder if there's some way I could motivate you to want to clean it up. I'm even willing to help, since liking a bit of cleanliness and order is my problem."

Fifth, never whip, hit, paddle, spank, beat, slap, cuff, pinch, or otherwise physically abuse your child.

Never.

Never send a child to bed without dinner, including dessert. (It would be interesting to know what percentage of adults with eating disorders had food withheld from them as children.)

Never punish your child through his or her body.

If your state allows corporal punishment of children in school, as thirty states do,* lobby your school board to stop it in your district and campaign to get it outlawed statewide.

When I speak out against corporal punishment in workshops, someone always says, "But, John, you have to spank a child who won't finally do what you tell him to. What else can you do?"

I respond, "In my experience, that's a question that's only asked by someone who was spanked as a child. May I ask, friend, if you were spanked?"

Always the answer is yes.

There are many reasons not to punish children physically, and no doubt you've heard most of them. The main reasons, it seems to me, are that corporal punishment suggests to the child that:

- Children are less important than big people and must put up with whatever big people do to them.
- The body is despicable and must suffer whatever the will wants to do to it.
- Violence is an acceptable last resort in a dispute between people who supposedly care for each other.
- Might makes right; bigger and stronger people are allowed to oppress smaller and weaker ones.
- It is permissible for individuals to take the law into their own hands and mete out punishment as they see fit.
- The adult beating the child thinks so little of the child that the adult is willing to hurt the child.
- The child is ungovernable except through the application of

*They are Alabama, Arizona, Arkansas, Colorado, Delaware, Florida, Georgia, Idaho, Illinois, Indiana, Kansas, Kentucky, Louisiana, Maryland, Mississippi, Missouri, Montana, Nevada, New Mexico, North Carolina, Ohio, Oklahoma, Pennsylvania, South Carolina, Tennessee, Texas, Utah, Washington, West Virginia, and Wyoming.

force and pain; therefore, to govern himself or herself in
future, the child will have to use force and pain.

From a social viewpoint, corporal punishment is evil because violence promotes violence. Beaten children beat other children; they
beat their children and spouses; they assault, injure, maim, and kill
other people. They are the main reason our nation is so sickeningly
violent.

Another important reason why adults shouldn't use corporal punishment on children is rarely mentioned, in part because adults dis-
count it, in part because adults (especially parents) fear it may be
true. This reason calls attention to the destructive power of suppressed
anger, as I am doing in this book.

*An adult shouldn't use physical or verbal punishment on a child
because such punishment will make the child angry at the adult.*

Of course, the child won't be able to express his or her anger,
because the adult has all the power and has convinced the child that
the punishment is right and the child wrong, defective, deserving to
be hurt and violated.

So the child will be forced to swallow his or her anger, turn it
back into himself or herself, and stockpile it with other suppressed
rage and pain—all of which causes the unhappy consequences we
spoke about in the first chapters.

Two excellent books spell out what happens to children who are
subjected to physical or verbal abuse by their parents: Alice Miller's
*For Your Own Good: Hidden Cruelty in Child-Rearing and the Roots
of Violence* (1983) and Philip Greven's *Spare the Child: The Religious
Roots of Punishment and the Psychological Impact of Physical Abuse*
(1991). If, as is likely, you were physically punished as a child, you
owe it to yourself to read Miller's book. If you have children, you
owe it to them to read both books.

Very briefly, Miller and Greven both say that children who are
hurt by their parents—either physically or psychologically—inter-
nalize an anger they cannot express against people they love. This
suppressed anger leads the children, as grown-ups, into neurosis at

the very least, and often into depression,* authoritarianism, and judgmental religiosity. It sometimes leads them into violence against
themselves (Miller describes the psychology of drug addicts, pros-
titutes, sadomasochists, and suicides) and violence against others.
(Miller gives the best explanation we will probably ever have of why
Hitler and the Germans who followed him killed Jewish people and
other "undesirables" without compunction.)

Children whose bodies, psyches, and selves are wounded are thereafter changed, especially if the wounding was done by their parents.
Some of the joy of existence is taken from them. "It is hard to love
life fully when one has been hit and hurt," Greven says.

From my own experience I know Greven is right. I was whipped
as a child—on at least one occasion whipped so badly I blacked out.
I often saw my sister whipped till her legs bled. Until I was in my
mid-thirties and learned how to get the rage and grief caused by this
punishment out of my system, I was an alcoholic, a drug addict, a
borderline depressive, an obsessive, and a might-be suicide.

Nearly all the problems that my sister and brother and I have
experienced as adults were caused by the parenting we received. This
parenting was abusive in many ways, but had it not included corporal
punishment everything might have been okay. Then, I think, we might
have escaped chemical addiction and despair.

If someone asked me what the first step is to a better world, I
would say, "Stop hitting kids."

The forces for corporal punishment are surprisingly strong. Parents
generally bring up children as they—the parents—were brought up,
and surveys indicate that probably four Americans in five were hit
as children. The Bible tells parents to punish their children as much
as is necessary to bring them to God. And, as Miller shows, using
violence to "break" a child's will is at the heart of the Western
tradition of child-rearing.

Can we change this? I think so. In my work I have found that as

---

*Greven: "Depression often is a delayed response to the suppression of childhood anger that
usually results from being physically hit and hurt in the act of discipline by adults whom the
child loves and on whom he or she depends for nurturance and life itself."

people learn fully to embrace their own feelings, they are more easily able to empathize with others'. I believe that no adult who has finally *felt,* acknowledged, and cried about the pain he or she suffered from being beaten as a child will beat another child.

Eighty percent of the men in my men's groups were beaten as children. Before they joined the group, eighty percent of those with children beat them. Once they've done work in a group—seen other men grieve the pain of their upbringing, learned to grieve their own pain—they stop.

I'm sure that in a hundred years people will look back at our treatment of our children with the same horror we now feel about Elizabethan England's disembowelings and drawings-and-quarterings, America's slavery and lynching, Saudi Arabia's 1977 shooting execution of a royal adulteress and beheading of her commoner lover.

My optimism is encouraged by what has happened recently in Sweden, a country with a Germanic, authoritarian tradition of child-rearing similar to ours and a country that often pioneers ideas for the rest of the West. In 1979 the Swedish parliament passed a law stating: "A child may not be subjected to physical punishment or other injurious or humiliating treatment." Though the law carried no criminal penalties, observers say it has transformed the way Swedes discipline their children. Because the society has ruled out violence against children, the Swedish people have found other means of discipline— boundary setting, discussion, reasoning, "time out," isolation, and the like.

You will find a way to discipline that is right for you. Only remember: it mustn't hurt.

WHEN YOUR CHILD IS ANGRY...

...encourage him, encourage her to express the feeling.

As I've said, young children do this naturally until they're punished for it. Children respond in the moment. When they are angry, they throw themselves on the floor and kick their heels; they shout, they cry, they rage. They don't "judge" their feeling—they feel it. They don't escape into their intellects and say, "Now, just a minute here. Obviously something is troubling me deeply, and if I think it through, I'm sure I can understand it so well I won't feel it anymore."

They get their feelings out through their body. Ten minutes later, they are whistling or playing a game or fretting about something else—anyhow, they are into a whole different set of feelings. They responded to their anger at the moment it occurred by relieving the stressful energy in their bodies, then quickly moved on.

You want to encourage your child's natural response. Certainly don't deny what he feels—by saying, for example, "You're not angry." You don't want to judge her feeling—by saying dubiously, "What are you angry about?" (Which means, "Give me a good enough reason, and maybe I'll let you be angry.") You don't want to shame or punish the child for feeling and for expressing the feeling—by saying, "You stop it! That's no way to behave. I'm ashamed of you. You used to be such a good child. If you don't stop, I'm going to send you to your room. Or thrash your bottom, so you'll really have something to wail about."

If the angry child is too young to understand what you're saying, embrace him, hold him, hug him, comfort him, talk gently to him. If the infant is having a tantrum and struggles to get free, put her down—gently, calmly—so that she can move, making sure that she can't hurt herself. *And then stay with the child,* leaning over him, so he can see you. Show that you love the child no matter how furious she is. Show that you can be *with* him in his anger, without judging or punishing him. Say things like, "Yes, yes, little one, you cry. You cry all you need to. I'm here. I'm not going away. I want to be with you, however angry you are."

When your child understands speech, say the same kind of things. And guide your child toward appropriate ways to express his or her anger, saying things like:

- "I can see you're angry. I want you to know I love you. I support you and your anger. Be just as angry as you feel."

- "Can you make an *ugly*, angry face? A face that shows how angry you are? Try it!...Oh, that's good. That's so angry!"
- "Take these crayons—the light ones or the dark ones or any ones you want—and draw me a picture of how angry you are."
- "Take this red plastic bat and hit that couch as hard as you can. . . . That's good! Hit it again and again, just as hard as you can." (Always praise the child's emotional release. Say, "That's fine! You're really hitting it hard. Hit it even harder if you want to." Don't say, "You're not hitting very hard. Can't you do better?")
- "Cry! Just go on and cry. That's the best thing to do. Get all your anger out. Right here and now. Keep crying till you feel better. I won't do anything. I'm going to stay with you, if you let me, so you know I support you and want to be close to you."

If the child is having a tantrum and tells you to go away, do so, saying something like, "Anger is tough, but I know you're going to handle it fine." Never punish—or praise—your child for having a tantrum.

- "Twist this towel as hard as you can, and put all your anger into it."
- "Scream into this pillow. No one will hear you—not that anyone is listening. Even I will hardly hear you. But I'll be here with you, because I want to be close to you."
- "Do whatever you need to to get rid of your anger—provided it doesn't hurt you or anybody else. The most important thing you can do when you're feeling angry or sad is to feel it and express it with your body so you get rid of it. But whatever you do or don't do, I'm going to love you, just as I always do, even if I don't always show you in the right way."

Imagine how different our lives would be if our parents had said things like this to us!

"But," you say, "what if it's *me* the child is angry at—you know, because I'm the parent?"

No sweat. That's perfectly normal. You're the disciplinarian—naturally the child's going to be angry at you.

This shouldn't change your message, just add a little to it:

- "I know you're angry with me. And I understand it. That's *fine*. You have a perfect right to feel whatever you feel. I love you just the same, just as much. You hit that couch as hard as you are angry with me, or twist a towel, or scream. I'm going to be right here with you."
- "I'll tell you how much I want to be here with you. I want you to squeeze my two fingers just as hard as you are angry. It won't hurt me a bit, and maybe it will help you feel that we're in close touch, even if you are angry with me. You'll be able to express the full power of your anger, but you won't hurt me and I won't hurt you."
- "I can see you're angry. Please, son, get it out. Do whatever you need to to get it out. Tell me how you feel. Tell your momma, too. Tell your sister. But get it out. Because if you don't, you're going to build up resentment toward me and your momma and your sister. And you'll have less room in you for love, compassion, and joy."
- "Are you angry with me right now? . . . I kind of felt you were. I'm really glad you admit it. I'd like to think you'd always feel you can tell me the truth, because you can. I'm not going to be hurt by whatever you feel."

Now, I know it will be hard for you to say these things to begin with. But remember, it will be even harder for your child to *accept* them and act on what you're saying.

Because it's new and different: a parent embracing his or her child's anger and inviting its expression. Children can be very conservative, and your child is almost certain to be embarrassed at first and for the first several times. That's okay. That's normal, given our culture. Keep trying. You are saying and doing the right things, and your child will feel better for them and be more likely to do emotional-release work because of your encouragement, even if not in your presence.

"But," you say, "what if my child gets angry when it's *inconvenient*? Like the woman in church whose five-year-old was cranky? What if I *can't* let my child express its feelings?"

Even when you think you can't, you often can. The mother could have let her daughter whimper in church—the child had only started and wasn't making much noise. If the girl continued longer than a couple of minutes, the mother could have taken her out of the room. Gently! Not jerking her up and dragging her off, the way it was done with most of us as kids.

Or the mother could have let her cry. Reporter Jimmy Breslin remembers what happened some years ago when Gloria Steinem was introducing the topic of sexual harassment in the workplace to a women's group at a Manhattan church.

A baby started to cry. The woman holding the baby tried rocking. The baby let out a real wail. The mother, sighing, embarrassed, got up to take the baby outside the hall, as mothers have been doing in churches and meetings and restaurants forever.

And up in front of the room, Gloria Steinem said, "Excuse me. Just stay here and let the baby cry. With all the noises we're subjected to in the course of a day, we should welcome the happy sound of one of our babies."

It was the first time that anybody announced from a stage that a baby's crying in a public room was a welcome sound of life. All the women applauded. It was only an aside during a day of vast importance, but this, too, would last. If the baby cries, smile and stay.

The first thing to say is, however inconvenient the child's behavior, never be cruel. Your first priority is caring for your child. It's all right to say "Shhhh" to a child, but with love, not recrimination.

If your child is very young—one or two or three or four—no one should expect her to have self-control. Let him fidget and cry. If she gets too obstreperous, take her away. Matter-of-factly—without roughness or shaming.

If your child is older and sounding off at a very awkward time— at a funeral, say, or a wedding—I'd recommend that you encourage him to contain his feelings for a little while. Whisper in your child's ear, "I know you're impatient, honey. But this will be over in a few minutes, and then you can shout all you want to."

If the event *won't* be over in a few minutes—perhaps you're at a concert or a play—don't tell your child that it will be. Instead, whisper, "I know you're bored. Can you wait till they're finished?"

If the answer is no, whisper, "That's okay, sweetheart. Come with me." And take the child outside, to someplace where she can shout and carry on.

A child is *never* at fault for feeling what he feels. If anyone's at fault, it's you. You thought your child might be old enough to be interested in the concert or play, or at least to contain her feelings till the performance was over, and you were wrong.

If your child *does* contain her feelings till an inconvenient event is over, then it is your responsibility, right away, to get her to release her half-suppressed feelings.

Don't say, "Wait till we get home tonight."

Say, "Son, we're going out to the car and get that anger out. Right now."

Say to the other adults, "My daughter and I will be back in a few minutes."

Say, "Go ahead, sweetheart—yell all you can. Nobody can hear us."

Say, "Rage all you want to, son. Get that feeling out of your body."

The point, always, is (1) to tell and show your children that you support what they feel, and (2) to encourage them to express their feelings, while making sure they understand that this expression mustn't hurt them or other people.

THE BEST WAY TO ENCOURAGE YOUR CHILD TO RELEASE HIS OR HER ANGER APPROPRIATELY...

...is for you and your spouse to have released *your* anger appropriately in the past.

I'm no psychologist, but I'm sure this is true. If our parents had displayed their anger, sadness, and, yes, their joy appropriately when we were young, we would now know everything we're struggling to learn from reading books like this and working with support groups and doing therapy.

Children imitate their parents. If they could grow up seeing their parents cry when they were sad and stamp their feet or shout or punch a pillow when they were angry—always without hurting themselves or anybody else—the children would think such behavior normal, especially since it is what the children themselves do naturally if someone doesn't shame them or shut them down. Furthermore, if the parents had empathized with and supported their children when the children expressed their feelings appropriately, the children would empathize with their parents and their emotions and draw closer to them.

But of course, this isn't the world most of us live in. In our present world, most children have learned by the age of four that they aren't accepted and embraced when they express certain emotions. They've learned, also, to fear their parents' expression of anger or sadness, because it brings on pain for them and others.

What can we do with *today*'s children? How can we retrain them so that they know they are welcome to express whatever they are feeling? And how can we, as parents, release our anger and sadness in ways that won't traumatize our children as our emotional expression has in the past?

All I can offer you here is common sense. We have to *talk* with our children. We have to tell them the truth. We have to say that big people don't know everything and that parents, even Mom and Dad, make mistakes. We have to explain to them, in terms they can understand, what emotions are, and that emotions are all good in themselves and bad only when they are expressed inappropriately.

Then we have to tell them that from now on we, their parents, mean to express our feelings—safely and appropriately, so that no one is hurt or shamed or made to feel bad—whenever we need to and can reasonably do so. We have to tell them what we will do (cry at supermarket openings, scream in the car, punch pillows, do joyful jigs) and assure them that we absolutely won't hurt them and, we hope, won't embarrass them, either.

If your child asks to watch you while you are releasing your emotions, say, "Wonderful! I'd love you to. I want you to see that feeling and expressing your feelings is good and something everybody should do, provided they don't hurt anybody else."

If your child is young, you will want to hold and hug him or her and repeat yourself a good deal and make sure the child knows that he or she is loved and is in no way the cause of your anger or sadness.

"BUT," YOU SAY, "WHAT IF MY CHILD *ISN'T* A CHILD ANY LONGER? . . .

" . . . What if I have a *grown-up* child?"

You do exactly the same thing: You support and encourage your adult child's feelings and their appropriate expression.

Adults are intellect-oriented, so your adult child will probably need more explanations than a young child would. Tell your adult child you read this book, *Facing the Fire*, and that it gave you a new way of thinking about anger and emotions.

If your child reads the book and agrees there's something to it, you could say, "Well, why don't we spend an hour doing some of the exercises it recommends? I know you're thirty-four, but it's never too late. *I'm* doing the blasted exercises, and I think they're doing me some good."

If your child says doing emotional-release work would be too embarrassing, by all means answer with the truth: "You bet it's embarrassing! That's part of the challenge—to see if we can break out of our rut and behave in a way that's truer to what we are inside."

Whether or not your adult child does anger-release work, he or she will sometimes be angry and expressing—or trying to express or suppress—his or her feelings. At all such times, be encouraging and nonjudgmental. Say, "I can see you're angry. Keep going for it. Get it out. That's great!"

If your encouragement makes your adult child angrier, that's fine. Say something like, "Be angry with me! That's *fine*. I'm *with* you, I love you, and I want you to get to your feeling and get it out."

In fact, your encouragement is very unlikely to make your child angrier. Nine times out of ten, the person expressing anger is grateful for encouragement and says so once the anger is out. The sweetest words I hear in my work as an emotional-release facilitator are, "Whew! Thanks for the support. I've never had it before."

Now, your adult child may try to get to his or her anger and fail. If this happens, say what I say to the people in my workshops who don't get to their anger:

"There is nothing to worry about. You're doing fine. You're telling the truth about your feelings. That's what we're working toward— not to be lying, not to be pretending, not to be pleasing other people with what we claim to be feeling. You're saying just what you feel. How many people do that? You ought to be proud of yourself for admitting you couldn't get to your anger.

"Just because you didn't get there today doesn't mean you're not going to get there next time. Or the time after. Maybe you had to be here today to be able to get to your anger next time. This isn't a race. Life isn't a race. Each one of us is working toward his real self or her real self. And that's what you're doing—working at just the right pace for you."

APOLOGIZING TO YOUR CHILD

All parents make mistakes with their children. They can't help it— they're people. People make mistakes.

People put their own needs and interests ahead of other people's, even when the other people are their children. People misunderstand other people and what's best for them, even when the other people are their children—maybe especially then.

When you realize you have made a mistake with your child, apologize. Take the child's face in your hands and say, "I'm sorry. Forgive me." And hug your child.

If there's a chance your child doesn't know what you're apologizing for, say what it is: "I'm sorry. Forgive me. I did"—whatever it was—"and I shouldn't have." Or, "I didn't do"—whatever it was—"and I should have."

You should apologize to your child however young or old the child is, and whether your mistake happened in the near or distant past. As you get deeper into understanding yourself and the influence upon you now of mistreatment that was done to you as a child, memories will come up of analogous things you did to *your* child. You will feel remorse and sadness for these things, and feel the need to apologize for them. You are apologizing not primarily to make your child feel better, though your apology may do this as well as show the child how to handle mistakes, but to make *yourself* feel better. You are apologizing to rid your body of shame and guilt and fear (of disclosure) and grief and anger at yourself.

If your child lives far away, you can write a letter or speak on the phone. It's usually better, though, if you can see the child and embrace him or her. Your message is the same: "Forgive me. I'm sorry. I didn't know. I didn't have the training or information I needed. If I had had it, I like to think I would have done better—paid more attention to you and your needs."

Explain specifically what you did wrong.

Your child may not want to hear, may try to let you off easy, or may not even remember what you did. "Protecting the parent" may be something your child learned from you—something you did for *your* parents. Say to your child, "I want you to know what I did wrong. It would make me feel better to get it off my chest. It sort of *stifles* me. And it's important for you to hear it too. It may help you better understand yourself and our family and how we act."

If your child still doesn't want to hear, respect that wish.

If your child doesn't accept your apology, if he or she says, "Screw you. It's too late," respect that feeling.

Say something like, "I'm sorry you feel that way, but I respect your feeling. I hate and regret the things I've done wrong and the wrongs I've done you, and I don't expect you to forgive me. I'm apologizing because I need to begin being at peace with myself.

"It's *fine,* your anger at me. I hope you'll feel your anger just as much as you can and find some way to express it, because I love you and want you to get that feeling out of your body."

Apologizing to your child improves your child's chances for psychic health, happiness, and a better relation with his or her own children. Like taking responsibility for your anger by screaming or twisting or pounding it out of you, apologizing to your child is a step toward breaking the ancient chain of child abuse.

A final point: If you as a parent have made your children suffer because of your compulsive or addictive behavior, no apology you make will mean much if you are still acting out this behavior. The best way to show your remorse is to get the help you need to change yourself and stop the behavior.

V
The
Benefits of
Anger

I'm getting ready to end this book now, and that makes me sad. I hate ending things, and I hate saying good-bye.

There! I'm glad I said it.

One of the important things that dealing with anger and grief has taught me is that I can feel and express any emotion I have in five or ten minutes and thus discharge it from my body, but if I run from the emotion, if I bury it to avoid feeling it, it can hang around for days. Weeks. Years.

So when I feel something,

- I need to *feel* it. Embrace it. Take it in—literally. Recognize it. Pay attention to it.
- And then, as fast as I safely can, *express* it. Which may mean shouting or singing or screaming or deep, deep breathing. Or telling someone safe about it. Or doing something in the world.

Suppressing a feeling has many sad consequences, but this may be the saddest: We spend endless hours evading an emotion we could deal with—feel and express—in a few minutes if we faced it.

If the emotion is a big one, it will probably return, perhaps later that day (maybe just a few minutes later), the next day, the next week, a couple of months later. When it returns, we deal with it again by feeling it and expressing it. Emotional health is a *process,* something we work toward but never finally achieve. All formulations of it are imprecise, temporary, and in need of further refinement and adaptation to particular circumstances. Life is open-ended, but since books aren't—can't be—they have to end.

I've spent this book saying things I believe are true and important. I hope I have answered your questions about anger and how to deal with it. Here is a brief reminder of what I have said so far:

A TEN-POINT SUMMARY OF THIS BOOK'S THEMES

1. Anger is a normal feeling.
2. Anger is an energy in your body that needs to come out.
3. You will feel better—"Ahhh!"—when you've expressed your anger (literally, pushed it out) from your body. You do this by safely losing control.
4. Running away from your anger—burying, suppressing, drugging it—is unhealthy.
5. Directing your anger at yourself is also unhealthy.
6. Your anger is yours, and you need to find appropriate, safe, and healthy ways to get it out.
7. Some appropriate ways to express your anger by yourself and with other people are suggested in this book.
8. Other people will not always welcome your expression of your anger or other feelings, but you will often need to tell them your feelings anyhow.
9. You may be able to help people you care about, especially your children, deal with their anger.
10. If you express your anger appropriately, it will increase

your energy, your intimacy with those you care about, and your serenity.

I'm going to spend our last chapter talking about Point 10, our new equation: *Anger, expressed appropriately, doesn't equal pain; it equals energy, intimacy, and serenity.*

18
The New Equation

Anger, expressed appropriately, creates energy, intimacy, and serenity.

ANGER AND ENERGY

Anger expressed appropriately increases energy because buried, blocked, inhibited, suppressed, or repressed anger is energy trapped inside us that has to be held down by other energy. When we get our suppressed anger out, we gain not just one but two new sources of energy:

1. the energy in the anger we suppressed
2. the energy it took to hold in that suppressed anger.

We probably don't gain that new energy *immediately*, as soon as we're finished discharging our suppressed anger, although this varies from person to person. Some people do feel the new energy as soon as they express their buried feelings. But more people start feeling the energy later the same day or the next day, or even the day after that, when they have recovered from their emotional-release work.

Because emotional-release work *is* work.

Emotional-release work itself uses a lot of energy because it has to break the bonds of habit, propriety, self-defense, self-consciousness, and self-control to liberate the feelings imprisoned beneath. Getting to those feelings and discharging them—"Arrrrgh!"—takes so much energy, it can exhaust you. It can make you feel cleaned out, drained, and definitely tired.

The biggest danger in emotional-release work comes *just after* it's over. You feel good, but you may also feel let down and empty. In our culture, what we're taught is, when you're empty, get stuffed. Put something into that emptiness, quick! Alcohol. Food. Drugs. Work. TV. Sex.

If your lover leaves you, get another lover—fast! If we're feeling a little low or bored, we've been encouraged to *do* something, look for excitement to take our minds off the problem. You've seen the bumper sticker: "When the going gets tough, the tough go shopping." The malls of America are full of people stuffing their emptiness with unnecessary activity and belongings.

Back when I was an emotional-release facilitator with individual clients, I saw the syndrome quite often. I remember working with a man who was his own boss, the head of a company, enormously self-disciplined. At our fifth or sixth session, much to his surprise, he suddenly got into his pain. The feelings he had been repressing came pouring out—rage, tears, sobs.

When the session ended I could see he was stunned. It was early afternoon, and I recommended he take off the rest of the day. Go home and rest; go for a walk by the lake. He said he couldn't do that. The people at the office counted on him.

Back at work, feelings from the session kept coming up, and he had to swallow them. He didn't get anything done. Then, as he was driving home, lo and behold, though he wasn't much of a drinker, he stopped at a bar for a quick one. Five margaritas later, they had to call him a taxi.

We spoke the next day. He couldn't understand what had happened. "I felt good after the session," he said, "but I felt empty."

Emptiness shouldn't be an enemy. Emptiness, as the Eastern religions know, is the normal human condition—nothing to fear. Emptiness is what makes selfhood possible. And individuality.

If, when you've done emotional-release work, you feel drained and empty, embrace the feeling. Hug it to you. You've come closer to your core. That's *you* you're feeling. If you can keep from running from that feeling, if you can be at peace just *being,* letting your thoughts wander where they will, taking good care of your body, getting rest and healthy food and whatever exercise feels right, the next day or the day after you'll find new energy starting in you, new emotions (maybe joy this time), a new sense of freedom and wholeness and potential in your life.

It's only normal: you'll feel lighter, elated, more at ease because you'll have gotten rid of pain you've been holding in. *Parade* magazine recently did an interview with Henry Nicols, a hemophiliac who contracted the HIV virus from a blood transfusion when he was eleven. Now seventeen, Henry has AIDS and has decided to go public about his condition in hopes of educating people about the disease.

When *Parade* asked him how going public had changed him, Henry answered, "I'm probably less irritable, because there's a big burden off my back now that I don't have to keep this secret anymore. So it's a lot less stressful. It's fantastic."

The stress of holding in his secret had diminished Henry's life. Getting the secret out brought him strength and joy. But, again: If releasing your suppressed anger, pain, and grief doesn't make you feel better right away, don't worry. Wait calmly; good things will follow.

If you *can't* wait calmly, if you're agitated, raging, or weepy, it means you haven't released all the feelings you need to at this time. You still have work to do now.

Psychologist James Pennebaker, whose work we spoke of earlier, has found that people who divulge their traumatic secrets at first feel worse than they did before they confessed, probably because they have relived their painful experiences. Shortly after confessing, though, the same people feel better, and for months thereafter their health, both physical and mental, is better than it was before.

Discharging suppressed anger is an important part of a larger program of *actualizing* ourselves—becoming who we really are, making what we show on the outside dovetail with what we feel inside. There is strong evidence that self-actualization leads to better physical and mental health.

Which means more energy—"Ahhh!" More strength for what we want to do—*umph!* More power of attention. More zest. More creativity. More bliss.

ANGER AND INTIMACY

Appropriately expressed anger creates intimacy because anger is an emotion, and intimacy is created by the safe sharing of emotions—*every* emotion, not just the ones we know people applaud.

Intimacy happens when a person feels, experiences, and expresses his or her feelings, at the moment they occur, with another person. Thus, every time we feel any emotion, including anger, we are offered an entrance into intimacy. We need only have the courage to report what we're feeling to another person—who, of course, we must *not* blame, shame, or criticize for what we are feeling.

Now, people are ready to believe this about most emotions, but not anger. "I can tell my wife anything," men tell me all the time. "I can tell her I'm sad, I'm lonely, I'm depressed. But I can't tell her I'm angry."

"Why not?" I ask.

"She won't be able to handle it. She'll be upset at the very least. She'll be scared. She might even *leave* if I let the whole thing out. I just can't."

There are four things I want to say about this.

First, let me emphasize that I'm talking about anger expressed *appropriately*. If we express our anger inappropriately—as 95 percent of anger is expressed—other people won't be able to handle it, and they shouldn't be expected to. If we blame, shame, frighten, ridicule, demean, or hurt the people to whom we're telling our anger, we're going to damage our communication with them, diminish our intimacy, even kill it.

Second, as I've said before, not telling our anger is based on fear—fear of abandonment; fear of not seeming to be kind and gentle and good; fear of anger, which our history has taught us to equate with pain; fear of the built-up, buried, denied rage in us, which we think we may not be able to control and which disgusts and humiliates us.

Third, not telling our anger diminishes our intimacy with the person we're keeping our anger from. As William Blake understood:

A Poison Tree
I was angry with my friend:
I told my wrath, my wrath did end.
I was angry with my foe:
I told it not, my wrath did grow.

Fourth, not telling our anger will sometimes provoke exactly what we fear. The wife leaves *because* we're angry and won't express it. She leaves because we're not sharing ourself with her. She leaves because there's a void at the heart of our relationship. Or if she doesn't leave, *you* leave, because you, the real you, isn't there and knows it. The wife was relating to your pretend self.

Before I understood how important expressing my anger was, I used to suppress it. I wouldn't tell my lover I was angry, and the instant I chose not to do so, I could feel myself pull away from her. She could feel it, too, though usually not strongly enough to speak about it.

Three or four days might go by. Then she'd say, "Are we going to get together again?"

"Huh?" I'd say, playing dumb. I could have won Oscars for playing dumb.

"Since Sunday you've been off somewhere else—anyhow, not

with me. What's the matter? Did I do something that made you angry?"

"Naw. Everything's fine. Nothing's wrong."

As I said this, I'd be thinking inside: "She'd be hurt. She'd get upset. She wouldn't understand. She'd think I'm a jerk. She'd say I 'shouldn't be bothered by it.' She'd think I was attacking her."

I was a coward. I didn't trust the validity of my feelings or the love and sensitivity of the woman I was with. I thought that anger had to lead to separation, as I had always seen it do.

But this isn't true. If a relationship is healthy (and if it isn't healthy, do we really want to be in it?), anger expressed appropriately will bring people closer. It will not only heal the angry person, but help heal the relationship too.

Say your lover is late picking you up and you're angry—excessively so. You realize a past buried anger has taken you over. You leave your lover a note and go off to deal with it by yourself, through emotional-release work and talking with friends, counselors, and support groups. Or say your lover turns up before you write the note and you two have to go on somewhere together. You say, "I'm real angry, but we're running late. Let's go—I'll deal with my anger later." You have registered your anger at your lover's coming late, but you've also made clear that you understand that the intensity of your anger is caused by past feelings, for which you're taking responsibility and which you're *not* going to dump on your lover.

Later, after you've dealt with your anger, you get together with your lover and say, "When you didn't come and didn't come, I got more and more furious. I have to tell you, I was beside myself. Being kept waiting or being stood up turns out to be a big issue for me. I see now it has to do with my childhood, naturally, and I want you to know I'm aware of the problem and I'm working on it. When I was a kid . . ."

And you bring the person you love into something deep within you that you've never previously revealed—maybe never previously realized.

Or say your feeling is present anger. You tell the person you're in a relationship with, "I'm angry. I'm angry, and I want to talk about it, if that's okay with you. What I'm feeling belongs to you and me in the present moment. I'm pretty darn sure of this because I'm not at all out-of-control angry. I want to tell you about it, in an appropriate way, hoping to grow closer to you. When I've told you, it will be out there for both of us to look at and *feel* and judge how true it is and what we're each responsible for.''

The way to intimacy is through self-revelation—of everything that's in us: anger as well as rapture, weakness and need as well as strength and delight. When we've told our anger appropriately to someone close to us, we've created more *space* in our relationship for love and tenderness and concern, because we've deepened our level of communication.

Since I've learned not to fear anger and learned to express my anger appropriately with people I'm close to, I can't count the times I've said something like ''I'm angry right now, and I want to tell you about it. When you do so-and-so, I feel . . . ,'' only to have the other person say, ''Gosh, I'm glad you told me! I hadn't known that made you angry. I'll do my best to do something about it. Thanks for sharing that.''

The same thing happens in my business life, though here the conversation generally goes like this:

Me: I'm angry. I want you to know it, and I want to tell you why I'm angry. You said that A, B, C, but now you're telling me that X, Y, Z.

Other Person: I appreciate you're being so frank about what you feel. I agree you have a right to be angry, and I will look into the matter and get back to you.

When one person takes the risk and expresses his or her feelings appropriately, two people are likely to move closer together.

YOU SHOULD *EXPECT* TO TELL YOUR FEELINGS...

. . . even if you're angry.

You should expect those close to you to support you, no matter what you are feeling, and to listen to you and love you after you've been angry in an appropriate way. If you don't have people in your life who love you and support you and let you be yourself, you have to ask yourself why, and make whatever changes you need to.

If you love someone, you should expect that person to support you—not in every instance, not in all your angers, but most of the time. They should certainly encourage you and be thankful that you're communicating your feelings.

A man, if he's heterosexual, should expect a woman in his life to support him in being angry appropriately and feeling all his feelings.

A woman, if she's heterosexual, should expect a man in her life to support her in being angry appropriately and feeling all her feelings.

Spouses should expect this from each other.

Homosexual men and women should expect this from their partners.

Partners, lovers, and spouses should support each other's feelings, but this doesn't mean they have to feel the same thing. They can support feelings without participating in them. They can be *with* the other person in sympathy while feeling whatever they feel.

If you don't have a supportive person or supportive people in your life, you may have to get angry enough about this fact that you take a hard look at your current relationships and, using your anger, a God-given energy, get out of what's stuck, dysfunctional, and less than satisfying and healthy.

Most of us didn't receive unqualified support when we were children, and because we didn't, the odds are that, as adults, we've chosen spouses and lovers and friends who are grudging in their support. We've built ourself the same box to live in because it's what we're used to. We feel comfortable when people aren't there for us and when we have to pretend to be what we're not to earn a sliver of approval.

Well, no more. Not for me. If people don't support me in my feelings, I don't want them in my life. Rather than stuffing my anger, denying who I really am, and feeling as if I'm home again performing for my parents, I prefer to be alone and be alive and provide my own support.

ANGER AND SERENITY

The root of serenity is self-acceptance and self-actualization. If we are not serene, it's because we are not ourselves. We are not ourselves because we weren't allowed to be ourselves with our families as we grew up. Our families weren't serene because the powerful people in them, the adults, lied and encouraged us to lie by keeping their real feelings hidden, often even from themselves. So there was always an underlying tension in the house. We walked around on eggshells, wondering if this or that parent was sad or mad, and if we should say or do something to head off an explosion.

Our parents punished us for trying to be who we were instead of who they wanted or needed us to be. We learned to hide our true selves and true feelings from others, and usually from ourselves. Thus we eventually became like the powerful people, "grown up."

The promise of self-actualization and self-acceptance is that, whatever our age, we can recover a portion of the self we lost, our true, spontaneous child-self. Until we do this, we will only be fitfully happy, momentarily content. Not serene.

This book is arguing that feeling our anger and expressing it are crucial to our self-actualization and hence our serenity. The goal in feeling and expressing anger is—"Ahhh!"—to be rid of it. Not to stay in our anger, but to release it.

Once we release our anger, we sigh. Phew, that's off our chest. Our mind and body are clear. Our problem may not be solved—it probably isn't—but our relationship to it has changed. We're over it for now. No doubt it will come back, or another problem like it, and we'll deal with it then. For now, we're singing in the kitchen as we do the dishes.

When we've released our anger, we've used it up. We've changed our perspective on everything. For a moment or longer, we've forgiven the world's unfairness, the cards we've been dealt, and the people who've hurt us. We've gone *through* anger to serenity.

We've been told that if we let ourselves get angry we'll never be able to forgive. I say just the opposite: If we get angry as many times as we need to and experience and express our anger as fully as we can, we'll move much closer to forgiveness than if we swallow our anger, hide from it, and deny it.

We've been told it's disrespectful to be angry at our parents, living or dead. In fact, if we're harboring suppressed, inhibited, or unacknowledged feelings toward our parents or anyone else, we are being disrespectful to them, because our deepest love for them is also buried. Were we to let out the rage and grief we feel toward them, our positive emotions would be freed. We'd come to remember the good things they did, memories that were lost when we shut down all our feelings toward them. Anger and grief are two paths that, followed long and hard enough, lead to forgiveness and serenity of spirit.

We've also been told that spirituality and anger are incompatible, because in Western religions, and to a lesser degree Eastern religions, anger is seen as an evil emotion. As I've said, though, anger isn't an evil emotion: It's a *human* emotion. I believe that by embracing our humanness—feeling our emotions, whatever they are, and expressing them and letting them go—we open ourselves to true spirituality. We have more energy for selfless endeavor, more patience to listen to others, more charity to forgive others (and ourselves), more humility to let others be as they are and stop trying to control them. We can have these virtues only when we have got our anger out.

Anger expressed appropriately, then, increases our serenity and our spirituality.

WHEN DOES THIS HAPPEN? WHEN DOES OUR ANGER TURN TO LOVE?

It can start today, if you start feeling your feelings and appropriately expressing them:

You have to study and get the skills. You have to be patient and go slow and look inside yourself and see what works for you. You have to practice—without practice, who does anything well? You have to make mistakes and try again. And you have to realize, deep as your bones, that turning your anger into love—like becoming yourself—is a lifelong process. It is never finished.

People want to believe that if they ever have the courage to confront their anger against their father or mother or sibling or spouse or child or ex-lover or boss or teacher or religion or whatever—if *finally* they get to the wrong done them and rage against it—that it will be done, gone, over *for good*. It won't. It will be gone for a while, perhaps a long while, perhaps a short while. A *layer* of it will be gone, and that layer will never have to be dealt with again. But if it is a big anger or hurt in your past, there will be other layers below, and life and thinking will bring them to your attention, and you will have to *feel* them and express their emotion from your body.

If you're like me and the people I've worked with, you'll find that you can usually express the new layers of feeling more easily and quickly, probably because you've seen that you can handle this feeling and are no longer frightened of it. In any case, even if layers of the feeling still remain in you—and who ever gets over the loss of a first love?—the feeling will no longer control you. You will be able to control it, exorcise it for the time being, and thus, to a large extent, control how you feel.

I wrote my first book, *The Flying Boy,* in my mid-thirties when I was finally beginning to realize—and feel!—the pain of my dysfunctional childhood, alcoholic father, and dependent mother. I wrote in a turmoil of rage and grief, a baseball bat on the bed beside my desk. When my memories got too strong to get out through my writing, I'd drop the pencil, grab the bat, and pound my fury into the bed until I collapsed in tears and exhaustion.

I did this every day for nearly nine months—months after the book was finished. Then one day I didn't feel the need to. What a surprise! The *next* day I needed to again, and the day after and the day after that. Gradually, though, I stopped. I still feel some anger toward my dad and mom, though nothing compared with the anger I felt before my work. But feelings come up. As I write about my parents now, I feel a pain in my gut—something I still need to deal with.

Emotions are like onions—there are a lot of layers to peel off. You work toward the goal of discharging all the pain, but you don't reach it. So you keep working. Your commitment isn't to perfection: It's to getting better. And knowing that you're fundamentally okay and, with ups and downs, are going to continue to get better is the bedrock on which you build your serenity.

You will find there are times in your life when you can do anger work of a deeply healing kind. At other times, your anger will be quiescent, and you'll be drawn to deal with other emotions.

Our emotions, being part of us, are natural and organic. There's some evidence they are seasonal. Certainly certain emotions appear at certain "seasons" in a person's life.

When the season comes for you to face your anger, the mother-lode anger you carry from your infancy and childhood, be gentle and patient with yourself, but do everything possible to work into your emotion as far as you can at that stage.

How long will you need to work? It varies. You probably won't be able to quit while you're feeling terrible. Feeling terrible is a symptom of needing to do more. If you find yourself saying, "I don't want to feel this shit anymore. I should be done with it," you still have work to do.

But don't force things. Treat yourself gently even as you work your emotions hard. You will know when you've done enough for the time being. A feeling of serenity—"Ahhh!"—will come upon you.

Perhaps you'll have been working for a year with an emotional-release group, and suddenly you find your cupboard is bare of things that outrage you. "Hey," you'll say, "I'm fine! I'm finished with this! Whew, there's nothing there. I feel great. Fabulous!"

You aren't finished. At best, you will still have to respond when life restimulates angers buried in you that you have overlooked or throws present annoyances in your path. At worst, the *same* angers you worked on will resurface.

Two years after you quit the group, you may find yourself saying, "I can't believe it. I'm *still* angry with my father. Was that whole group for nothing? I thought I had cleaned Dad out of me. What is this?"

It's another layer of your feelings. This anger book, that workshop, a third twelve-step meeting, your fifth therapist, Iron Andy's Wildpersons Emotional-Release Week Plus Outdoor Survival School—they're all good, but insufficient.

Nothing—that is, no one thing and not everything taken together—will heal you permanently of anger. Or pain. Or grief. Or guilt. Or any of the dark emotions.

You can't be healed because you're alive (thank God) and human—with many layers of emotion in you, and subject to the endless ills and pleasures of our kind. You can't be "fixed" because you're not broken. (Anyhow, feelings don't need to be fixed: they need to be felt.)

You can't be healed of your feelings, but you can learn how to live more easily and openly with them, so that the darkest of them passes quickly over and away, like the shadow of a summer storm across the land.

A SHORT GOOD-BYE

I am deeply grateful to you, reader, for sticking with me all this way. I've learned a great deal I hadn't known—or hadn't known I knew—while trying to explain my ideas to you. I end the book even more confident than when I began it of the importance of our feeling and expressing what is in us.

May we have the courage to become more and more fully who we are!

And may we find people with whom we can safely and fully share ourselves! Including our anger.

John Lee's Audiocassettes

Why Men Can't Feel and the Price Women Pay
Expressing Your Anger Appropriately
Grieving, a Key to Healing
Healing the Father-Son Wound
What Co-Dependency Really Is
Addictive Relationships
Saying Good-bye to Mom and Dad
Couples, Caring, and Co-Dependency
The Flying Boy: Healing the Wounded Man Series

If you or your organization would like to sponsor a John Lee workshop on Anger, Men's Issues, Adult Children, or Relationships, please call 512-478-5971.

For information on lectures and workshops with John Lee, contact him at:

> John Lee
> West Austin Station
> P.O. Box 5892
> Austin, Texas 78763
> (512) 442-7992